ACCOUNTABILITY
CL⬚CK

ACCOUNTABILITY
CL⬜CK

A GUIDE TO **ACCOUNTABILITY** IN WORKPLACE

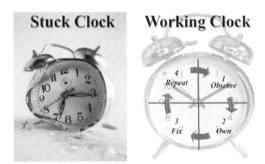

*A practical approach to get over "chalta hai" attitude
and achieving enhanced levels of Individual,
Company and Country Accountability*

Authored By

● **Paramjit Singh** ● **Sandeep Kaul**

**WINGS
PUBLICATION**
WE GIVE WINGS TO YOUR DREAM!

Publisher's Disclaimer

WINGS PUBLICATION
WE GIVE WINGS TO YOUR DREAM!

Registered Office- 907-Sneh Nagar, Sapna Sangeeta Road,
Agrasen Square, Indore – 452001 (M.P.), India
Website: http://www.wingspublication.com
Email: mybook@wingspublication.com

First Published by WINGS PUBLICATION 2021
Copyright © PARAMJIT SINGH & SANDEEP KAUL 2021

Title: *ACCOUNTABILITY* CLOCK
Price: INR 599 and USD 12
All Rights Reserved.
ISBN 978-81-948673-7-1

LIMITS OF LIABILITY/DISCLAIMER OF WARRANTY

Hello!

We get it. You picked up this book on *Accountability*, knowing that:
- either you
- or someone in your team at work,
- or your company leaders,

Are struggling with *Accountability at Workplace.* You can relate to the image of a *Stuck Clock* but are looking for help on how to make it work. What you have in your hands (or on your digital screen) will show you how to uncover your unique talents and gifts, and turn those into action, so you can take up a job that makes you happy without the fear and anxiety of not being Accountable.

You or people around you want to become Accountable but are struggling to figure out how to do it? Is there a step-by-step approach? How other successful people or companies achieve it? Because of this, you see yourself like a *Stuck Clock*, whereas you want to look like a *Working Clock*.

THIS BOOK IS FOR YOU
- If You are trying to find what is *Accountability*.
- If You want to make real changes in the way you and your team work
- If You're going to be someone who does what they say they're going to do.
- If You would like to learn how to stay Accountable for your tasks and goals
- If You want different results than you've ever gotten before

Following the method shared in this book will help to lift the fog, uncover the best of yourself and use that to get into action so that you look like a *Working Clock* and get Accountable. The problem is that many of us only follow the set path like a robot.

Following steps in this book, you will learn to place yourself and all of your gifts at the centre of your confident self. You will be able to use this approach to make progress and to find meaningful, fulfilling Accountable state.

WE'VE BEEN THERE.

You want to move faster and not having enough time in the day to do all the things on the To-Do list. Yet at the same time lacking real fulfilment at work. The first step in creating what you want is to get reconnected to how you want to feel. The whole point of being Accountable and hold others Accountable is to feel satisfied at the end of every day and live the life you want to live. In this book, we will share with you different stories of success and failure for you to observe the difference it makes to be on the *Stuck Clock* side or the *Working Clock* side of *Accountability*.

Because you are unique, special, and you have something to offer to the world that no one else can.

OUR PROMISE TO YOU

The 4 step *Accountability Clock* framework will transform your thinking about being Accountable. You will appreciate the knowledge of the external needs and what you need to do to be satisfied and successful.

This book, with the help of the *Accountability Clock* framework, will help you move from *Stuck Clock* situation to becoming a *Working Clock*. Supported with real stories from different companies and people, you will be able to discover the secret success sauce of *Accountability*. We have also used the epic Mahabharata to showcase the winning and losing behaviours. As you progress from one step to the next, there are quick exercises for self-evaluation and reflection. These exercises act as a mirror to your progress.

EACH CHAPTER OF THIS BOOK INCLUDES:

1. Opening and Closing with the epic Mahabharata for context setting
2. Self-evaluation exercises
3. Corporate, individual and social stories for you to pick up the action points to understand and implement the concept of *Accountability*.

WHAT IS NOT INCLUDED?

We know how quickly you would like to shift to the *Working Clock* mode from *Stuck Clock*, but we also know that behaviour shifts take time, energy, effort and courage. So, if you are looking for a quick *Fix* solution, 2-minute solutions, this book may not help.

If you are looking for someone to handhold you in this *Accountability* journey, this book will be a useful companion to you. We also offer individual and group coaching services so that you can become Accountable by following our step-by-step approach.

About the Authors

Paramjit Singh and Sandeep Kaul have collaborated for many projects together over the last eight years. They have worked on projects ranging from Coaching, Learning & Development, Leadership Development, Assessment Centres, Human Resources, Sales Productivity enhancement and Corporate Videos. They compliment each other with their different skill sets to create Win-Win client outcomes.

After successful careers with leading companies like Tata Group, Mahindra Group, Monster.com, HT Media, ICICI Bank, HDFC Bank, MetLife and BNP Paribas, they created a niche for themselves supporting companies and startups become future-ready. Together, they have helped 110+ companies in business strategy, people development and corporate film production engagements. Their experience gives them the edge to create a solution that not only meets but exceeds client expectations.

Both Sandeep and Paramjit come with their distinct experiences of more than two decades each. Sandeep has extensive experience in setting up and scaling large size corporate divisions, including establishing business divisions from the startup stage and running a consulting firm since 2012. Paramjit, on the other hand, has rich corporate and consulting experience spread across multiple functions and geographies.

Sandeep has a strategic outlook, while Paramjit has operational and hands-on experience. Together, they bring a great deal of authenticity, conviction, clarity and passion to their consulting engagements. This combination provides the best solutions for their clients. Their collective experience of working on multiple projects together has given them the advantage to complete complex projects together.

Preface

As a societal culture, we feel India has lived long enough to be following "chalta hai" (it's okay) attitude. Perhaps, the colonial rule of over two hundred years has left a behavioural imprint that if not me, somebody else will do it. We tend to follow this at home, company and society in general. Indeed there are many exceptions to this behaviour among the Indian corporates. Many individuals have risen above their surroundings to prove that circumstances cannot define their destiny. This book is about finding the core elements that separate the victims of the circumstances from the achievers.

We unravel the secret sauce that makes the super achievers be on top of their game. What makes Tata Group, Nestle, Eicher Group and many others achieve the pinnacle of success. How they can shed the "chalta hai" attitude and stand up to be accountable? *Accountability* remains one of the essential ingredients towards the success of an individual, company or nation. Until everybody takes up their own, their company's or India's *Accountability*, we would remain a nation that 'could have' been on top of the global rankings.

This book provides practical, actionable steps to come out of the victim mindset and become accountable. We have also drawn inspiration from the 5000 years old epic Mahabharata. These examples are only to explain and understand if we are still living in that era. How the critical characters in Mahabharata failed in their *Accountability* that led to the greatest war in India's recorded history. Blending the old with the new, we have also covered real stories from highly successful companies that have inculcated *Accountability* as a culture and how they are benefiting from it.

We hope that you enjoy this book. The tools for *Accountability*, how to evaluate *Accountability*, how to imbibe it and what can be done for higher *Accountability* are all covered in this book. We hope that this book helps you build *Accountability* in the workplace and the environment around you.

During writing this book, quite a few people asked us, "What made us write this book?", and we always responded with Mahatma Gandhi's words, " Be the change that you want to see in this world".

We invite you to join our community in building *Accountability* at the workplace.

Paramjit Singh
Sandeep Kaul

Acknowledgments

O ur collective experience of 50+ years in owning P&L responsibility at firms as well as consulting engagements has made us identify one difference that separates the successful from unsuccessful, i.e. *Accountability*. Especially in the Indian context, where '*chalta hai*' (its okay) is entrenched as an acceptable behaviour. A lot of people remain in the victim stage for their life and are not able to achieve what they want. This book is a must-read for such people. The framework covered in this book can help people come out of the victim cycle and take charge of their careers, companies and the nation.

We have referred to the Indian epic Mahabharata, and the entire construction of the concepts is supported by characters and situations from this epic to construct this book. We want to acknowledge the various individuals, corporates and publication that we have referenced in our book. We took inspiration from *The Oz Principle-Getting Results Through Individual and Organizational Accountability*, written by Roger Connors, Tom Smith, and Craig Hickman and published in 1994.

We are thankful to our publishers Wings Publications for advising us during the research stage as well as the publication stage.

We want to acknowledge our family members and friends who not only helped in providing suggestions but also critiqued the book whenever we requested and supported us through this journey. A special gratitude to Tanmay Trehan for giving his valuable input.

Foreword

Paramjit and Sandeep have started a conversation on the most important aspect of leadership that is *Accountability*. A lot of leaders today have authority and responsibility but can genuinely do better when it comes to outcomes and *Accountability*. *Accountability* is not only what we do, but also what we do not do, for which we are accountable. The *Accountability Clock* is a timely book for a post Covid era, it was relevant pre Covid but is even more relevant post Covid where *Accountability* has taken many dimensions. The *Accountability Clock*, through a four step framework helps you measure, improve and calibrate *Accountability*. Whether you are a CEO, or a team leader or someone who leads teams this book is a must for both entrepreneurs and intraprenuers. As a wise person said "At the end of the day we are accountable to ourselves. Our success is a result of what we do"

So pick up the *Accountability* Clock and make it part of your manual for delivering meaningful outcomes.

Dr Annurag Batra is a Much Below Average (MBA) person who is trying to stretch 24 hours to 48 hours every day. Dr Annurag Batra, is founder exchange4media and Chairman BW Businessworld, an author, a TV show host, an angel investor, media expert and a serial entrepreneur.

Index

PART

I

Understanding the *Accountability* Context in our Society

CHAPTER

1

How *Accountability* is Lost and How to Regain It

SETTING THE CONTEXT

Mahabharata is one such story that has varied shades of people, and even after 5000 years, it continues to fascinate both young and old generations. It makes people ask themselves how different players in the story played out their roles. It captures the journey across 3 generations, how some of the characters are already aware of the power within and how some like to grab it with deceit, force, sympathy, and rightfulness.

While the whole story is fascinating, the sub-story, Bhagwat Gita, lessons from Krishna to Arjun about his *Accountability* define the difference between right and wrong. How stepping away from responsibility will never end the war. Krishna says the whole purpose of him taking a human form is to *Fix* the wrong with the right through Arjun. That 45 minutes conversation makes Arjun acknowledge that if he doesn't stand up to the occasion, somebody else will. Krishna tells him that he would take action himself if Arjun runs away.

There is more than one character in the story that tries to run away from *Accountability*. Typical of many people, even today. How Mahabharata characters quickly passed on the responsibility to others and blame circumstances. Many characters came in contact with Krishna, but only Arjun was chosen to demonstrate real ownership.

How the doyen of the clan, Bhishma allows himself to remain focused on his own pledge while allowing all the wrongs to happen in front of him. How the blind king, Dhritarashtra, takes solace in the fact that it's only his son Duryodhan, who is the right custodian of his crown. How a crafty and devious uncle, Shakuni, lays out the plan to fulfil his purpose while fronting Duryodhan.

How Yudhishthira's misplaced sense of *Accountability* trapped him with a false sense of Dharma, as he understood in childhood from various saints and Bhishma. How Karna's sense of *Accountability* towards Duryodhan blinded him to follow the wrong side. How Dronacharya, the spiritual guru evaded his *Accountability* in overlooking the ambitions of Duryodhan.

People relate to the story from ignorance to knowledge, from fear to courage, from insensitivity to caring, from paralysis to powerful, from victim to *Accountability*, because it appears, so true. Unfortunately, even the most ardent admirers of the story often fail to learn its simple lesson, never getting off the righteousness, blaming others for their circumstances, and waiting for miracles to happen and make all the problems disappear.

Today in 2020, Gen Z is seeing how the families, societies, workplaces, governments, leaders are all becoming victims and staying away from taking *Accountability* for their acts.

IDENTITY CRISIS IN INDIA

In today's India, the sense of *Accountability* has eroded to such an extent in our culture that everything has become someone else's job. When confronted, the most straightforward response is *"we are helpless, the power of taking action lies somewhere else"*. The sense of *Accountability* and ownership that was evident when the whole nation fought for independence. Today, *"chalta hai"* (its okay) appears to have taken over society. We as a nation need to reclaim our sense of *Accountability*.

The independence of India in 1947, sowed the seeds of nationalism. People, including millions of refugees, took an oath to make India a great country. However, as the years went by, more and more Indians started looking for excuses for not doing what they are supposed to be doing. People became insensitive to building a society that helps each other.

Even for the fundamental civic responsibility, the Indian PM had to sensitize people on the importance of keeping their surroundings clean through the Swachh Bharat (Clean India) mission. People, in general, remain insensitive to their essential civic responsibilities, leave aside taking ownership. Generally, people felt that anything that's outside their homes; they are not concerned about it. Be it driving habits, breaking traffic rules, throwing garbage anywhere, spitting, and even honking near sensitive places like schools and hospitals. These are some of the examples of how we display a lack of *Accountability* on daily basis.

Another trait of low *Accountability* is the blame game. "Oh, we are born poor, what can we do". "There are no good schools around". "We are busy earning a living, how do we imbibe good civic habits in children". "Our parents could not provide us anything". "We are victims of our circumstances". "We have no power to take any decision". "We can't help, decisions come from the top". "We have done our job, don't know where the file is stuck".

We are writing this book in the backdrop of the raging Covid-19 pandemic. There are numerous examples of how political leadership across Indian states and the world has blamed the situation on different factors. However, there are very few examples of state leaders who stood up, took charge, and did whatever they could do, to be Accountable in the situation. The same story played out across the world. Many great countries have blamed one or the other thing for the situation that has got created. While the blame game is on, media the fourth pillar of democracy is rushing to quench our thirst for sensationalism. It is serving us 24x7 the images of failure, stories of despair, exposing the very private moments of loss, and grief.

Pain has become a business. Like we witnessed in the media circus that ensued after the Nirbhaya case (a young girl gang-raped, brutally violated, and finally died in the Indian capital). There was a competition to prove who adjudicated their responsibility. Years later, one of the leading OTT platforms showcased how an individual in Delhi Police rose to the occasion, spent sleepless nights, fought political pressures, and achieved the case closure by arresting all culprits. This case proves that quite a few people love sensationalism without looking if somebody is doing their duty with complete *Accountability*.

While the Nirbhaya case reached its logical conclusion, not all do. The public, in general, likes to see the sensational side of issue. Very rarely, the focus goes towards the few who silently own up and follow the path of *Accountability* and ownership. Some of the notable examples that come to mind are Ms Neelam Katara (mother of Nitish Katara, who was murdered). Ms Sabrina Lal (sister of Jessica Lal who was murdered). Ms Neelam Krishnamurthy (mother of 2 children who died in a Delhi cinema fire tragedy).

The "blame game," as well as the seemingly unquenchable "thirst for exposure," are just two symptoms of a widespread "responsibility avoiding" syndrome, which, not surprisingly, has afflicted business organizations as well. The majority of people in organizations today, when confronted with poor performance or unsatisfactory results, immediately begin to formulate excuses, rationalizations, and arguments for why they cannot be held Accountable, or, at least, not fully Accountable for the problems.

We can witness a similar attitude in the executive. Most of the elected leaders invest considerable time in finding ways not to be held accountable. They make systems and laws so that their actions remain protected. If we look at how many political leaders have faced jail term in the last 72 years of independent India, we find that the figure is quite low. These are the same political leaders who make huge promises, present poll manifestoes, shout in public rallies during elections. Once they get elected, most of them conveniently forget what all they are responsible for doing—the whole focus shifts from doing to evading. When youth see these political leaders, lot of them mistakenly feel that's the way to be successful.

Decades of appeasement for vested interests, political leaders have created schemes and welfare measures that promote the victim approach. Instead, if the focus would have been on meritocracy, there would have been many more successful leaders in society. India would have been a different country altogether. Even in the current Covid-19 crisis, the focus perhaps is more on appeasement instead of providing employment opportunities.

Another interesting data is the percentage of taxpayers amongst adults in India. Only 4.18% of adults pay income tax in India, (source: Income Tax Department, NSSO). 4.18% is the pre-COVID figure, and we have to wait for some more time to see how the pandemic has impacted the taxpaying population and the tax collections. If the schemes get launched to feed more than 61% population for eight months, without them doing anything it would put an extra burden on those who are paying taxes (e.g. Pradhan Mantri Garib Kalyan Anna Yojana).

So, what is the *Accountability* expected from the government of the day? If governments continue to feed more than 61% population with the contribution from only 4.18% population, the obvious conclusion is not far. If we are not making people responsible for themselves, how do we make them accountable for others? For decades reservations quota has remained a discussion point. Everybody knows how it's misused. But, being a political hot potato, nobody would like to touch it. How do we bring responsibility to citizens when they see that people born in a particular caste can get an advantage in education, jobs, and promotions? We have to move to a society of merit from a culture of reservation. At the same time, reservation systems serves as an excellent tool to provide opportunities to the scheduled castes, tribes, and backward classes so they can compete with others having more privileges. Unfortunately, the system has instead created a generation of people who grew on their birth benefits instead of meritocracy.

KEY TAKEAWAY

The majority of people in organizations today, when confronted with poor performance or unsatisfactory results, immediately begin to formulate excuses, rationalizations, and arguments for why they cannot be held Accountable, or, at least, not fully Accountable for the problems. If we analyse the industry, we again find many examples. The toy industry in India went down to Chinese imports because they were cheap. The IT industry could not make any world-class product because we do not invest in R&D. We lost our edge in garment exports because other Asian countries' labour is cheap. And the list goes on. So, instead of introspecting and taking up the responsibility, we come with excuses.

Yes, there are exceptions to this situation, ISRO (Indian Satellite & Research Organisation) is a shining example of our world-class abilities. The organization works on frugal budgets, offer world-class solutions, and has never shied away from taking up the responsibility of failure.

BLAME IT ON OTHERS

Let us look at three specific examples for a better understanding of "*blame it on others*" syndrome.

CASE STUDY : SATYAM COMPUTER SERVICES

The Satyam Computer Services scandal was one of the biggest corporate scandals of its time in 2009, in which its chairman Ramalinga Raju confessed that the company's accounts had been falsified. The scandal size was Rs.7,000 Crore (US$ 1 bn).

SEBI and stock exchanges were informed by Ramalinga Raju on January 7, 2009, through an email, wherein he accepted inflating the cash and bank balances of the company. Raju's famous statement

11

that "he was riding a tiger and did not know how to get off without being eaten" cut little ice with authorities. Satyam's position was quite good as Raju mentioned in an interview that they have a cash balance of Rs 4,000 crore (US$ 550 mn) and could leverage it further to raise another Rs 15,000-20,000 crore (US$ 3-3.75 bn). Satyam was the fourth-largest IT Company at that time. Ramalinga Raju was convicted with ten senior management members and two partners of PwC, on April 9 2015.

The takeover by Tech Mahindra: The government of the day had to order auctioning of the company in the interest of investors and 50,000+ employees of Satyam Computers. Tech Mahindra took over from Satyam and eventually merged into the parent company. Satyam fraud turned out to be worth Rs. 12,320 Crore (US 1.65 bn) and a case of financial misstatements as per SEBI's probe. 7,561 Fake bills were detected in the company's internal audit reports and surprisingly furnished by a single executive. These counterfeit invoices pushed the company's revenue upward by Rs 4,783 crore (US$ 637 mn) over 5-6 years. Not only fake invoices but fake debtors were also reported to the tune of Rs.500 Crore (US$ 66 mn) in a probe that lasted 5-6 years. Nobody could ever imagine that such a large and respected company of its time would indulge in such an irresponsible, fraudulent, and criminal conduct.

CASE STUDY : KINGFISHER AIRLINES

Vijay Mallya floated Kingfisher Airlines with an ambition to become an industry leader with a superior and differentiated offering. Soon it garnered a large share in the aviation market with a vast number of destinations and numerous awards to its credit that depicted a innovative picture for the company.

Excellent customer feedback, coupled with excellent flying experience helped Kingfisher achieve success in a short period.

Towards the end of 2011, Kingfisher Airlines plunged into a massive financial crisis. Many private and public sector banks provided loans to Kingfisher Airlines thanks to the reputation of the UB Group and its CMD. The time came where Mallya had to fly out to the United Kingdom, leaving many public sector banks with unpaid loans, thousands of employees with unpaid salaries, thousands of vendors with unpaid bills, and hopes of so many families came down crashing.

Let us examine some issues that lead to the failure of a successful airline. Strategically when the airlines were competing, fuel prices were going north, acquiring a low-cost airline, dented its premium image. One operator cannot afford to offer a 'luxury' experience, too many changes at the top management, and owners at the helm without the knowledge of running an airline. All this led to the company having a financial situation that was beyond salvage.

CASE STUDY : SAHARA GROUP

In the year 2010, the Sahara group started raising funds from the public under the names "Housing Bonds", "Nirmaan Bonds" and "Abode Bonds". They used their registration papers from the Registrar of Companies as false approvals from the SEBI and the RBI. According to SEBI rules, an unlisted company can accept deposits from two hundred shareholders in a financial year through private placement. However, Sahara Group raised money from 3 Crore (30 million) investors. In 2011, SEBI ordered the group to refund this money to investors with 15% annual interest. The Supreme Court upheld this order.

Raising a sum as large as Rs.24,000 crores (US$ 3 bn) from 3 crore (30 million) people was bound to raise red flags from the regulatory authorities. The company could not provide legitimate details and valid identity proofs of the investors when asked by SEBI. This ambiguity made the regulatory authority suspicious of money laundering. SEBI asked Sahara to refund investors because it felt Sahara was raising money in violation of capital raising norms and few sections of the Companies Act. The tribunal ordered the company to refund the money to the investors, which it was unable to do.

On February 26 2014, the Supreme Court of India ordered the arrest of Subrata Roy, Chairman, and founder of Sahara India Pariwar (family), for failing to appear in court in connection with the Rs. 24,000 crore (US$ 3 bn) deposits which his company was unable to refund to its investors as per a Supreme Court order, after a legal dispute with the Indian market regulator SEBI (Securities and Exchange Board of India).

An arrest warrant was issued against Subrata Roy. The Supreme Court had ordered his arrest, and he surrendered immediately. SEBI asked him to pay Rs.10,000 crores (100 billion) as compensation. Sahara has had problems raising the money, and as of today, Subrata Roy still remains a resident of Central Jail. Since Sahara hasn't been able to deposit Rs. 24,000 Cr with SEBI, the Supreme Court had asked Sahara India to submit a bank guarantee for Rs. 20,000 Cr. In July 2015, SEBI cancelled Sahara's mutual fund license - it ordered the cancellation of Sahara Mutual Fund's certificate of registration on the expiry of six months. This landmark judgment is a milestone in India's corporate landscape.

KEY TAKEAWAY

If we study the above three examples, they first appear as if it's not their fault, it's circumstantial. That's what all three promoters used as an excuse. However, another view is that in all three cases maybe a Duryodhan was at play. Someone who was raised with false expectations to become the king one day, who compromised all ethical norms of conduct. Someone whose only objective was to win irrespective of the means. As eventually in all three cases, there came a time when they had to face reality. Despite having an enviable successful business position, their desire to keep rising, pinned them down.

THE ACCOUNTABILITY CLOCK CONCEPT

Well, if we don't find answers in the present, we need to go back in history to learn. How do we ensure that we do not end up in a situation similar to Mahabharata? Who could be today's Krishna to show the right path to Arjun?

So what separate Duryodhan & Arjun? Do Arjun's of the corporate world also need a Krishna to show them the mirror and compass to make them stay on the right course? A thin line separates success from failure, the great companies from rest.

As we embark on the journey of understanding the successful behaviours and defeatist behaviours, we would like to use the analogy of a *Stuck Clock* and a *Running Clock*. We will use the four quadrants of an analogue clock that's working as a metaphor and how going in clockwise direction, successful people can achieve outstanding results.

The *Stuck Clock* has excuses, blaming, confusion, helplessness, while *Working Clock* has a sense of reality, ownership, commitment, solutions to problems, and action. Losers who tend to languish like *Stuck clock*, create stories explaining how things went bad to worse, winners reside like *Working Clock* are driven by values, righteousness, commitment, and action.

You can visualize the difference between *Stuck Clock* victimization and *Working Clock Accountability* in the below diagram.

KEY TAKEAWAY

Most of the organizations find themselves in a *Stuck Clock* situation whenever they have to avoid *Accountability*, consciously or unconsciously. The easiest thing that comes to their mind is the feeling of being a victim. This victimization continues until they are finished. The only way they can save themselves from oblivion is moving to a *Working Clock* framework. That's the way to survive and thrive. Till the individual, team, organization, or country stays like *Stuck Clock*, unaware and unconscious, things become difficult to the point of no return. Stuck in this situation, they quickly resort to a pattern of denial, rejection, blame, helplessness, dodge, and fret.

CASE STUDY : SACHIN TENDULKAR AND VINOD KAMBLI

If this process goes unchecked, it can have both individual and professional implications. We can think of a cricketing example when two friends joined the Indian cricket team. One went to become the God of cricket, and the other followed the victim path.

According to cricketing great, Kapil Dev, "Indian batting legend Sachin Tendulkar and his childhood friend Vinod Kambli, started their cricketing careers together and they both were good. People say that Kambli, maybe, was more talented, but his support system, the environment at home, and his friend's circle were different than what Sachin had. Later on, we all know what happened. Sachin continued and played for 24 years, and Kambli just disappeared as he failed to live up to the triumph he achieved early in his career".

They put on a world-record unbroken partnership of 664 runs in a school match. Kambli, who started his international Test career three years after Tendulkar, impressed everyone with his knack of scoring big runs. He scored a double century in only his third Test match against England and followed it up with another double ton in the next Test he played against Zimbabwe.

However, Kambli, the precocious talent soon faded away because of inconsistency and a lack of discipline. Kambli played his last Test match in 1995 and his final ODI in 2000. Despite being immensely talented, Kambli played only 17 Tests and 104 ODIs in national colours.

Whereas, his childhood friend Tendulkar went on to become one of the greatest cricketers of all time. Sachin had an illustrious international career that lasted nearly 24 years, and during the span of his career, the master-blaster created umpteen records.

Perhaps, Kambli operated with a *Stuck Clock*, and Tendulkar moved like a *Working Clock*. Kambli possibly could not handle success as it was sheer talent brilliance. Tendulkar, on the other hand, worked his way up, step by step. Kambli had to struggle much more with his mental state while Tendulkar was in control of his mindset.

THE MIND GAME

How mind control can create havoc is highlighted via a survey published in Business Standard newspaper (May 2020). The survey shows that a whopping "93% per cent corporate employees are anxious to return to office after the corona virus is contained and the lockdown is relaxed". While a majority, 59% are concerned about their health, 25% said they are anxious about their financial situation.

In comparison, 16% feel that the crisis will be elongated, and this uncertainty leads to high anxiety. There is enough evidence to suggest that engaged and secure employees are far more productive in performing their jobs better, while those under stress perform worst. Does this pandemic situation of 2020 give a wake-up call about being overly alert of the people who are like a *Stuck Clock*? So, can we say Duryodhan succumbed like a *Stuck Clock*? Well, the answer won't be that easy, we have to wait for some more time.

HOW DOES ONE GET TO *WORKING CLOCK*?

As the diagram shows, one has to take the steps in the order depicted on the right side of the diagram. Start with *Observe, Own, Fix,* and then *Repeat*. This approach would help you *Own* up, and that's the first step towards *Accountability*. This approach would help you get out of the "victim mindset".

The first step - *Observe* is for you to start recognizing and acknowledging the whole situation i.e. see the actual reality. You would soon realize that this perhaps is the most challenging step. How many people, including yourself would be honest in looking "under the carpet"?

The second step *Own* means accepting the realities and accepting that what can be done by you. This *ownership* usually comes hyphenated with *Accountability*. What can we do better will only come by receiving constructive feedback? How many people would accept that there's a scope of improvement in what they are doing for years? The second step, *Own* can only be possible if the first one is successful.

Only if people accept that there's a scope of improvement, they'd be willing to *Fix*. This third step would make people plan for action. People would start to look for better solutions that they thought never existed.

The last step *Repeat* means having a plan to ensure that whatever solution is arrived at; it is implemented and periodically reviewed. Now, these four steps may appear as common sense, and that's what makes people shift permanently to *Working Clock*.

WHY IS *ACCOUNTABILITY* UNAVOIDABLE?

We may try all different ways for rejecting it, avoiding it, blaming others, play helpless, dodge it, or fret it; but we will have to accept the *Accountability* and own it up, Period! While there could be some days we may not be okay, we may have personal priority, overwork, but eventually, that *Accountability* would stick with us. We have to accept the instruction in the retail shops that say, "you break it, you pay for it" as a metaphor. Deep down, we know that nobody except us owns the direction that our life takes and how do we manage our lives. This is our responsibility. End of the day, it's the results that matter.

If we study any modern management principles of total quality, employee engagement, customer delight, leading by example, focus, everything boils down to *Accountability*. *Accountability* makes people personally responsible. It makes people rise above their limits and get the results at any cost (without compromising integrity of course). Organizations worldwide are struggling with this as a number one challenge of people not being Accountable and dodging their responsibility.

While it is a widespread 'disease' across companies, very few know how to build and sustain it. Given the pre-COVID-19 economic situation and the current pandemic situation, it is further leading to "it's not my fault" syndrome. While some may have compromised integrity to reach the pinnacle of their businesses, as discussed previously in three case studies, eventually it leads to the collapse of not only their companies but also creates a tremor in the industrial sectors they belonged to. They left thousands of people jobless. It also left many people wondering if that's the way to grow?

Many people at one or the other time use the excuses like; "I didn't have enough time". "If we only had the resources," "The schedule is too tight," "That's not my job," "It's the boss's fault," "I didn't know," "The competition outsmarted us," "The whole economy's in trouble," "Things will get better tomorrow."

All these justifiable words only support our thought process on "why it can't be done," instead of "what else I can do." People do fall victim every day to unreasonable bosses, unethical competitors, manipulative colleagues and pandemics.

Indeed there are many things in life over which we do have control. Sometimes, people become victims of other actions, like employees of three companies we discussed previously.

But even then, they just cannot move to the *Working Clock* without following the 4 steps shared in this book. They can't live in an unfair, powerless, victim, blame game environment forever. They have to begin to turn things around until they take charge of their circumstances and accept their responsibility for better results in the future. They must get to the *Working Clock* that separates success from failure.

WHAT YOU CAN EXPECT FROM THIS BOOK?

✓ In the first chapter, we looked at the societal context vis-a-vis *Accountability*. In the three case studies shared in this chapter, we saw how people use their victim behaviour to justify inaction, excuse ineffectiveness, or rationalize poor performance. They unwittingly stifle their progress.

✓ In the later chapters, we will demonstrate how people who accept *Accountability* for making things better, move beyond their victimization to overcome obstacles, deal with setbacks, and rise to new heights. By the end of this book, readers would be in a position to learn how to become accountable for results and how to create cultures that develop and reward the sort of *Accountability* needed to build the Indian corporate character.

✓ This understanding of the seriousness of our current situation will help you tread the real path to results, and you will be able to differentiate the subtle, often obscure, line between circumstances and *Accountability*.

✓ On our journey, we will look at real examples from the business world to detail precisely how people and organizations/ groups, with a focus on *Accountability*, can overcome the obstacles, excuses, and circumstances that keep them from getting the results they want.

✓ We will analyze the startling as well as eye-opening experiences of individuals and groups in a wide spectrum of organizations. We will demonstrate how people in organizations overcame the victim mindset and circumstantial situations to move to the *Working Clock*, to attain superior performance.

✓ During the journey, we will refer to situations/stories outside of organizations and what made those stories become shining examples of *Accountability*. We will focus on the fundamental cause of poor quality, low productivity, customer dissatisfaction, inefficiencies, wasted resources both human and otherwise, non-cohesive teams, or a general lack of *Accountability*. We aim to push the envelope beyond the organization sphere and develop *Accountability* as an attitude that makes your and country's future brighter.

✓ Once you are able to distinguish *Stuck Clock* attitudes and behaviour from *Working Clock* performance, you'll be able to find yourself being able to tap the transforming power of *Accountability* for not only yourself but also your organization. We assure you that the journey would be worth the time and effort to address such an important issue.

CHAPTER

2

The Sufferer Mind-set

THE 'VICTIM' DURYODHAN, REALLY?

There is and always will be a debate if Duryodhan of Mahabharata was a victim of his father's aspirations, or his uncle Shakuni's, revenge against Pandava's or his own choosing. People remember him as a devious, greedy, power-hungry, and unethical person.

It is essential to understand the difference between being a victim of circumstances and of their own choosing. Duryodhan is the second most celebrated villain of Indian mythology after Ravan from the epic Ramayan. Duryodhan is depicted as greedy, disrespectful of his elders and friend Karna, tactless, cold-blooded, and seems to have no good qualities in him. He relies heavily on Shakuni, is greedy towards the crown, acts like a coward, disrespects Bhismpitamha and his parents and treats his best friend Karna as an object by using him now and then. But he was not a completely bad person as depicted in Mahabharata.

He had many good qualities. He never disrespected his parents or Bhismpitamha. He was whimsical and sometimes forced his wishes on his parents threatening suicide (in dice game too, he insists on playing again). He was a loyal friend of Karna, and their friendship is one of the most impressive points of the epic. He never condemned Karna for being a lower class born child nor disrespected him. The friendship between Karna and Duryodhan can be an example of friendship and loyalty even in modern times.

He strictly sticks to his duties as a Kshatriya. He never ran away from combat even though the Gandharvas arrested him, and even in his last battle during the Kurukshetra war, he fights bravely. He chooses to face Bhim in combat over all the other Pandavas, whom he could have easily defeated in action, is much more skilled in mace fighting. Duryodhan is tactless and relies on his uncle Shakuni on every plan and cannot even make plans of his own without failing poorly at them. Bhismpitamha never hated Duryodhan. When Duryodhan is dying, he accepted his defeat and the mistakes he had committed, including Draupadi's (Krishna's sister) disrobing, saying it was wrong of him to order Draupadi's disrobing, however, Yudhishthira should not have gambled his wife.

In the future chapters, we will go deeper into understanding behaviours of people who are in *Stuck Clock* like Duryodhana. We will understand how those behaviours impact them and the world around them.

Dr Stephen Covey, in his best-selling book, 7 Habits of Highly Effective People, says that effective and successful people challenge the circumstances. Effective and successful people believe that it's their own choices that make up their life. Thousands of people in courts of law every day plead innocent playing the victim card. Mercy pleas get filed on account of health, age, safety, gender, religion, minority status, economic status, and what not. Victimisation has impacted our society, from small inconsequential acts to life-destroying abuses, that it affects everyone, every day. The agony a person wrecks on another, poses one of the challenging dilemmas of current life. Many people and organisations can fall prey to victimisation.

THE DIFFERENCE BETWEEN *ACCOUNTABILITY* AND VICTIMISATION

So, what separates *Accountability* from victimisation, there's a fine line that separates going around your circumstances to get the results you want or falling into the victim cycle where you can simply get stuck.

Remember this difference is permanent, but the stay is not permanent on either Clock, and neither individuals nor organisations can stay on the same Clock between these two realms because events will inevitably push them to own or otherwise. It is okay for both people and organisations to exhibit *Accountability* in some places yet exhibit victim behaviour in others. Some areas or circumstances will influence them to think and act from either on *Working Clock* or Stuck clock perspective. There would always be situations that will not prevent you from ever failing like a Stuck clock. One can't perfect that humanly. Even the highest achievers, can get stuck in the victim cycle at times, but the ones who are accountable cannot remain there for long.

Those living like *Stuck Clock* people or organisations consciously or unconsciously avoid *Accountability* for results. They will move through predictable stages in an unending cycle that prevents individual and organisational productivity:

- they appear ignorant or pretending not to know about their *Accountability*
- claiming it's not their job
- evading their responsibility
- blaming others for their mess
- quoting confusion as an excuse not doing what they are supposed to do

- asking others to tell them what to do
- claiming that they can't do it
- developing their story for why they are not at fault
- finally waiting to see if some miracle will give some hoped-for miracle

THE MOST TRUSTWORTHY COMPANIES CAN ALSO FAIL SOMETIMES

Tata's earned the distinction of the trust through the values by which the Tata group and its companies operate. 66% of Tata group's shares lie with charitable trusts in the Tata's holding company, Tata Sons Ltd. The profits from the group companies help the trusts to cater to broader societal needs.

Arun Maira (former board member Tata Motors, Member Planning Commission of India, and Former Chairman Boston Consulting Group, India) explains the Tata Group and its brand value. The extraordinary faith of the Tata brand and its values, 50 years ago saved him from quite an embarrassment when he returned from his first overseas travel in the year 1969.

International travel was limited during those years. The Reserve Bank of India (RBI) used to allow carrying a small portion of foreign exchange, that too only for a limited period. Even imports were restricted: travellers were allowed only INR 500 worth of goods on return. After spending seven days in Singapore on a business trip, I was returning, with the allowance of £60 for everything including boarding, lodging and local travel.

The expectation from friends and colleagues was for me to bring something in return from Singapore. Having left with little money after all spends, I bought a lot of cheap toys and ball-pens as gifts from a Chinese shop.

At the customs clearance counter at the airport on return, the customs official emptied the whole bag. This action made everybody in the customs queue quite amused. Soon, the amusement became irritation when the customs official asked me to show the bills to satisfy him that the complete stuff is worth less than Rs500. Fortunately, his senior officer intervened and asked; "What is the problem?" Now the official who emptied my bag said that "this man says all this stuff costs less than Rs500!" The customs officer asked me "Where do you work?" I replied "Tata Steel". Hearing this, the customer officer told the other official that if he says this stuff is less than Rs.500, it must be so. People at Tata's never tell a lie. Hearing this, the official started to put the things back in the bag.

Almost a decade later, when I was with Tata Motors, another Tata group company another anecdote brought home to me how Tata's had earned their reputation as trustworthy partners.

In the 1970's, for the first time, Tata's set up their foreign production facility for assembling commercial vehicles in Malaysia. This facility was a joint venture with the Malaysian partners. This JV Company's bankers decided to recall their loan since the company struggled to make a profit. After giving a final notice to their partners in Malaysia, the chief executive officer of the bank, who was an Australian, came to Mumbai to issue a final warning to Tata's. His mandate was clear "put in more money, or the company would have to be closed down".

Owing to RBI's restrictions, Tata's were unable to remit any more money, and this would impact Tata's reputation. Therefore, Tata's instead of assuring any more money gave a letter to confirm that they would send some more managers to turnaround the company. Unconvinced, the banker wasn't sure about the value of the Tata's letter. He knew the people at Deutsche Bank, Germany.

He also knew that Tata's have a joint venture with Daimler Benz of Germany, so he decided to check with Deutsche Bank. What he heard from them was that a note on a Tata's letterhead carries more value than any financial guarantee.

Now, why would Deutsche Bank have such respect for Tata's brand? Mr Maira shares another story. While he was in Malaysia to turn around the company, the chairman of that company invited him to meet the directors of KraussMaffei. KraussMaffei, a German engineering company, who were in negotiation with the chairman of the Malaysian company for another JV. When he met German directors, and they got to know that he was from Tata, they shared why they trust Tata and what does Tata brand mean for them.

They shared a story that in 1946, immediately after World War-II ended, and they met the Chairman of Tata group, Mr J.R.D. Tata with Mr Sumant Moolgaonkar (ex CEO of Tata Motors, erstwhile TELCO) at the bombed Munich railway station. Owing to the situation, no Indian company could sign any legal agreements with Germans since India was still under British rule. German directors requested if Tata's can take their best technicians with their families to India since they are out of work. They promised that these technicians are outstanding in metalworking and they can teach all they know. That's all they wanted. This proposition opened up an opportunity for Tata's to learn from the best in the world. Once India gained independence from British rule in 1947, the directors received a letter from the Tata group. It stated that owing to India's independence, Tata's can now pay for the technology and services of their technicians and requested to quote the price. The German directors went on to share that this letter has become a legend in their company to understand what trust means. It demonstrated how to honour the debt even if it is not demanded or expected or legally binding.

We should remember that watertight contracts between the two sides do not gain trust. Doing the right things always build trust. Very often, leaders and organisations that often say, "Trust us. Surely you know who we are", may not be perceived to be fair and transparent. Those who value trust, they don't say but show. Trust is a slippery slope: hard to climb, easy to slide down.

THE NANO STORY...WHAT WENT WRONG?

The Tata Nano was the crown jewel of Tata back in 2009; it was Tata's Tesla Model 3 in the sense that it was Tata's effort in bringing a car down to a ridiculously low price to make it accessible to everyone. But Tata's project was way bigger!

The Nano was Tata's dream! It launched with a base price of just INR 1,00,000 (US$ 1300) making it the cheapest produced car in the world. Tata's triumph lead to the making of documentaries. But Tata in 2009 did not know that the Nano's woes were about to begin!

Mediocre Marketing – Marketing was not Tata's cup of tea back then, and the marketing was less than up to the mark for this car. A car priced this low needs adequate marketing to cover costs while advertising.

Tata went full steam on their marketing initiatives, but they focussed on using the term 'cheapest'. Unfortunately, the car launched in a time period, when we were using the word 'cheap' as a metaphor to denote the low quality of something. This perception created a stigma that caused the public to perceive the car as inferior, which it certainly was not!

Tata invested a lot of money into this project. They engineered an entirely new engine, a two-cylinder unit, and built the Sonnad plant in Gujarat primarily for the Nano.

Now, these costs are quite typical for a car in general. But when this car is priced so low, the margins are wafer-thin; hence recovery of investments is solely dependent on the volume of sales, which is dependent on proper marketing.

Tata also made another error by launching the INR 100,000 variant as the first car launch. This approach caused significant issues in production, as sales initially skyrocketed for the base model. Tata could have waited and slowly released the base model of the Nano a few months after the launch of the car. This delay would have given them time to stabilise their production and remove the build quality issues the car initially had.Consequence – The Nano failed to create a niche for itself. This gap meant that the Nano appeared as a rival for the Alto, the highest selling car from the number one passenger car manufacturer in India. The problem was that Nano undercut the Alto so heavily in terms of price that it features and engine did not stack up against the Alto. The Nano, however, was the value king. It received immense praise from the journalists for its stellar value. But the public seemed to have a different opinion, as the Alto's sales soared, while the Nano's sales slowed.

The Nano was supposed to help budget bike buyers' work their way up to owning a car. A bike alone cannot fulfil the needs of a family. Tata's then Chairman, Mr Ratan Tata mentioned the reason to launch this car was that he saw a middle-class family of four riding precariously on a bike, and decided to give the pride and safety to this segment.

What did Tata's do? – Tata's ended up embracing the competition and changed its target audience to young, urban car buyers. This change was evident in 2013-14, with the introduction of new variants in the top-end.

Tata launched the Nano Twist variant with power steering along with an ad campaign that had the cars running on the building walls. Its main selling point became its Nano size, and not its price now. This improved sales but only marginally. Unfortunately, all of these factors slowly brought the sales of the Nano to the zero mark as of January 2019.

Conclusion – The Nano was Tata's most ambitious project. Tata managed to achieve the unthinkable! Tata surprised all of their competitors, and international brands with the Nano because this project was so big, but the margins were incredibly small. Eventually poor marketing, low sales lead to the demise of this project!

TATA NANO: *ACCOUNTABILITY* FAILURES

1. Tata did not come up with a unique financial strategy for the Nano
2. The marketing campaign launched initially slowed down sales for the Nano
3. The corporate communication could not counter negative media coverage that further slowed down sales for the Nano

These factors hindered the Nano's sales heavily, slowing the growth of the car

The Nano story tells us that even the most reputed and trusted brand can get beaten down by lack of *Accountability*, resulting in a *Stuck Clock* with an estimated loss of about Rs.1000 Crore (US$ 150 mn) !

SIGNS THAT YOU NEED TO UP YOUR *ACCOUNTABILITY* GAME

The first requirement to start the *Stuck Clock* is to acknowledge that you're functioning like a *Stuck Clock* and paying a high price for it. Once that acceptance sets in, you begin with *Observe* attitude that gives you the perspective you need to get to *Working Clock*. Often, unable to overcome the inertia of the victim cycle on your own; you need feedback from an objective person such as a friend, spouse, or, as in the case of Nano, a customer.

However, one can significantly improve the ability to recognise when you become stuck in the victim cycle by looking for one or more of the following suggestive clues:

1. You feel "held caged" by your circumstances.
2. You sense you have no control at all over your present situation.
3. You become deaf to feedback direct or indirect.
4. Customers think you could have done more for better results.
5. You start finding people for blaming and pointing fingers.
6. You discuss more of problems and what you cannot do, instead of what you can do.
7. You overlook the most demanding issues you are facing.
8. You find yourself avoiding to ask questions about your *Accountability*.
9. You feel you are being viewed unfairly and you can't do anything about it.
10. You often find yourself defending the situation.
11. You discuss more things you cannot change (e.g., company, situation, economy, government regulations).
12. Your confusion stops you for not taking action.

13. You skip people, meetings, and situations where you report on your responsibilities.
14. You take comfort in saying:
    - "How am I responsible?"
    - "I couldn't have done anything about it."
    - "Nobody told me."
    - "We'll play it by ear."
    - "Tell me exactly what you expect me to do?"
    - "I would have done it differently."
15. You get into "boss or colleague bashing" thus wasting a lot of time.
16. Your deploy energies in narrating a story for explaining the reasons for not doing.
17. You ace the story of deception for doing it.
18. Overall, you see the world as hopeless.

TIME TO ACT

The moment you find any of the above signs, in yourself, your team, or your organisation, you need to act straight away to help yourself, or someone else recognises those justifications for what they are: barriers to *Accountability* and ownership and compromising results. After you become conscious of this situation, you and others can begin to understand the distinctions and intricacies of the victim cycle.

SIX STAGES OF THE VICTIM CYCLE

STAGE ONE

1. *Reject: The most crucial and common thing found in people/ organisations like Stuck Clock is to Reject / Deny / Ignore the sign of a big brewing problem.* There could be many reasons for that response; a few common ones are:

   a. *It's not a problem until it's a problem for many. Why should I bell the cat ?*

   b. *Hoping the problem would evaporate*

   c. *I'll have to explain the reason for the problem*

   d. *I am too junior to be heard*

   e. *My senior also saw and kept quiet*

   f. *What do I benefit in raising it, I only lose*

   g. *I don't have a solution for it*

CASE STUDY : CHERNOBYL STORY

There are many examples in world history on the impact of rejecting the early warning signs. Sometimes the cost of denial is incomprehensible in dollar and time terms. Let's discuss the most recent human tragedy on the face of the earth, denying/ rejecting/ignoring early warning signs when the Chernobyl accident happened.

Early hours of April 26, 1986, brought the world's worst nuclear catastrophe in the known history. The whole of Europe with a large part of the globe witnessed radioactive clouds spreading after an explosion in Chernobyl nuclear plant in northern Ukraine. The impact was similar to that of 500 Hiroshima bombs as the explosion released 50 million curies of radiation in the atmosphere. Curie is a unit of radioactivity used in the system of radiation units. This explosion led to evacuation of 50,000 locals from the city of Pripyat, located a few miles away from the explosion site.

The then Communist Party of the Soviet Union General Secretary, Mikhail Gorbachev received a wakeup call early morning at 5:00 a.m. on April 26. He received a message that there had been an explosion and fire at the Chernobyl nuclear power plant, but the reactor was intact. Gorbachev himself remembered many years later that in the first few hours and even the first day after the accident there was no knowledge that the reactor had exploded and that there had been a substantial nuclear discharge into the atmosphere.

Ideally, this would have called an emergency session of Politburo, but Gorbachev decided not to disturb other members of the Politburo or spoil their weekend. Instead, he allowed the creation of state commission to enquire the causes and how to deal with its outcomes.

At that time Boris Shcherbina, who was deputy head of the Soviet government and chairman of the high commission was called from a business trip to Siberia and sent to Ukraine. April 26, 8:00 p.m., he arrived in Prypiat that was eighteen hours after the explosion. Prypiat town had a lot of construction workers and operators of the nuclear plant. Until Shcherbina arrived in the city, there was hardly anything done for bearing the consequences of the disaster.

Local Soviet hierarchy was not prepared to take any responsibility to declare the reactor as dead. Only after Shcherbina started brainstorming with the local administration, it emerged that unthinkable has happened. They concluded damage of reactor core because of the meltdown, and the radiation has happened all over the place.

IN PRYPIAT, RADIATION RISING, BLAST IMPENDING AND VACILLATING OFFICIALS.

The first challenge was to ensure that the reactor fire should be put off and stop it from producing more radioactivity. Officials kept exchanging ideas. As a leader, Shcherbina suggested sprinkling water on the reactor. He understood from scientists that it would further aggravate the nuclear fire. Sprinkle sand, came another idea. But how to bring sand to the reactor, came another challenge. Shcherbina used his authority to line up a military helicopter and few chemical experts to reach Prypiat.

While the brainstorming was going on, immediately after 9:00 p.m., the damaged reactor got activated again causing three more explosions. The explosion was powerful enough to turn the night sky into the red sky with red-hot pieces of fuel rods and graphite flying the air. One of the commission's expert said "It was a striking spectacle" as he observed it from the third floor of headquarter of the Prypiat party, housing the high commission. They could see the worst-case scenario playing out in front of them.

During the commission members brainstorming, the experts could envisage that the situation may lead to a chain reaction of disasters. The first explosion only confirmed their fears, and they were fully aware that this is just the beginning of the chain reaction. Still, they can only wait since they do not have many choices. Even if no new explosion took place for some time, the last one created havoc. The wind speed picked up, and it started covering the north of Prypiat city with the radioactive clouds. When checked for an update, the radiation level had shot up to 320-330 micro roentgen from earlier 40 per second. Roentgens is a legacy unit, measuring exposure to electromagnetic radiation.

One of the directors of Moscow nuclear-power research institutes, Armen Abagian, who was sent to Prypiat as part of the government commission, contacted Shcherbina and asked for the city be evacuated. He remembered that children were running in the streets; people were hanging washed clothes out to dry, while the whole atmosphere was radioactive. He and his colleagues had to take shelter under a metal bridge while returning from the accident site.

Every expert familiar with the radioactive leaks knew that the town has to be evacuated. Still, the Soviet regulations formulated in 1963, specified that the civil evacuation would happen at a 75-roentgen. Every expert knew that with the speed of spread, it wouldn't be far when eventually it has to be ordered, but nobody was willing to take that call against the threshold norms, to order the evacuation.

SLUGGISH ADMINISTRATIVE RESPONSE

When people realised that the decision-makers are dithering, they began leaving the town. The city administrators snapped the intercity telephone networks. People working at the nuclear plant were prohibited from sharing news of what had happened with their friends or relatives. Soviet citizens always relied better upon family and informal networks that had always served better than state-controlled media. The same network got quickly activated in Prypiat, circulating news about the nuclear-plant accident within hours after the accident.

People in the Prypiat town started to understand that a disastrous accident has happened in their backyard. They were stopped by police to turn back. They saw a covering of the roads with foam-like material through water tankers. By afternoon people could see the arrival of the military with their carriers.

They could also see the military planes and helicopters filling the sky. Police and military personnel were wearing gas masks and respirators, but children were returning from school without any protection. Children were given some tablets in the school and advised to stay indoors.

People began to be more alarmed by the evening. They could smell the metallic smell. A lot of people did not wait and started to leave the town. At the same time, there was no official information on what had happened and what to expect. Soldiers were patrolling the Yaniv station where people could get trains to Moscow.

FIFTY MINUTES OF EVACUATION NOTICE

By midnight on April 26 scientists managed to convince Shcherbina to order an evacuation. But they knew that Shcherbina's decision required senior level approval. Scientists tried speaking to a couple of secretaries to order the evacuation. The secretaries could only provide sympathy and not the required order. Finally, Shcherbina phoned his boss, Premier Nikolai Ryzhkov. He told him that Prypiat needs to be evacuated. Immediately. Ryzhkov understood that the radiation in spreading full speed, while people in the town were experiencing it full blast. So, finally, he decided to start evacuation from tomorrow. Trains and buses were prepared. People were advised to take only the bare necessities. Shcherbina ordered to prepare lists of citizens for evacuation within two hours by local administrators.

The levels of radioactivity in Prypiat started rising quickly. On April 26 it was in the range of 14-140 mill roentgen/hour. Next morning, April 27 at 7:00 a.m. it had risen to between 180 and 300 mill roentgen. Some areas that were close to the nuclear plant, it reached an astonishing 600 roentgen. Officials taking evacuation non-seriously pushed the early morning evacuation to early-afternoon evacuation. For some people living in Prypiat, the evacuation came as anticipated, but for others, it was a shock. Prypiat city radio made the announcement soon after 1:00 p.m.

Local radio started blurring "Attention! Attention! In connection with the accident at the Chernobyl atomic power station, unfavourable radiation conditions are developing in the city of Prypiat. To ensure complete safety for residents, children first and foremost, it has become necessary to carry out a temporary evacuation of the city's residents to nearby settlements of Kyiv province. For that purpose, buses will be provided to every residence today, April 27, beginning at 14:00 hours, under the supervision of police officers and representatives of the city executive committee. The recommendation is that people take documents, necessary items, and food products to meet immediate needs. Comrades, on leaving your dwellings, please do not forget to close windows, switch off electrical and gas appliances and turn off water taps. Please remain calm, organised, and orderly."

This radio message got repeated four times, but many still did not understand the seriousness of the situation. People with families were in a large shopping centre that was full of parents and children eating ice cream. Since it was a weekend, people were taking everything nice and comfortable. Even 36 hours after the blast, people did not have reliable information about it, and mostly they left on their own. There was nobody to suggest people on how to protect themselves and their children.

In contrast, Soviet laws were clear on triggering the automatic public warning, after reaching a particular radiation level. That danger level had already arrived in the early hours of April 26. But it was ignored by one official after another. Eventually, thirty-six hours later, people were asked to gather their belongings and wait on the street for about 50 minutes before the start of the evacuation.

IN 2020 ALSO THE ACCIDENT'S HARMFUL IMPACT IS STILL FAR FROM OVER!

The evacuation got over by 4:30 p.m. same day. Officers were eager to report it to Moscow. Shcherbina called at lunchtime on Sunday; he told Premier Nikolai Ryzhkov: "There are no people left in Prypiat. There are only dogs running around." Since people were not allowed to take their pets, a few days later, the police created special squads to kill both stray and pet dogs. But not just canines who were remaining in Prypiat. About 5,000 employees of the nuclear plant also stayed to ensure that the shutdown of the other reactors takes place as planned. Young couples enjoyed their parents' departure to have their apartments to themselves. There were some elderly who decided to stay behind. Since they did not understand why they should leave when the planned evacuation was for three days only, unfortunately, they did not know they would be leaving forever.

The evacuated people carried not only their irradiated bodies but also their contaminated clothes and personal belongings to their temporary homes to nearby towns and villages. Next day of the evacuation, KGB officials informed Ukrainian party authorities that about 1,000 people who evacuated, had moved to towns and villages of nearby Chernihiv oblast on their own, 26 had reported to hospitals with symptoms of radiation-related sickness. KGB was busy suppressing the spread of rumours and unreliable information. However, they could do nothing about the circulation of radiation. After the evacuation of Prypiat and nearby villages, the buses went back to Kyiv. They started on their regular routes, resulting in the spread of high levels of radiation around the city of 2 million.

THAT WAS JUST THE BEGINNING.

Central party leadership of Kyiv refused to cancel May Day parade that was to be attended by the huge number of people, including children. The party leadership was very well aware of the increasing levels of radiation. Hundreds of thousands of schoolchildren were eventually evacuated from Kyiv as well. While just a few dozen people died as a direct impact of the explosion and radiation poisoning in Chernobyl, the World Health Organization puts the number of cancer deaths related to Chernobyl at whopping 5,000. An area over 50,000 square miles contaminated in Ukraine, Belarus, and Russia.

Thirty years later, in April 2016, the world marked the 30th anniversary of the disaster. People breathed a sigh of relief as the half-life of caesium-137, one of the most harmful nuclides released during the accident, got over. This isotope was the longest "living" isotope of caesium that could affect the human body through external exposure and ingestion. There were other deadly isotopes present in the disaster that long passed their half-life stages. However, the accident's harmful impact is still very much alive. Tests revealed that the Cesium-137 around the epicentre, Chernobyl is decaying much slowly as predicted. Some scientists believe that the isotope will continue to damage the environment for at least 180 years! Other radionuclides will possibly remain in that region forever. Last note, the half-life of plutonium-239, detection of which was found about 1200 miles away in Sweden, is 24,000 years!

STAGE TWO OF VICTIM CYCLE

2. *Avoid: The second stage in the victim stage of Stuck Clock is to Avoid. This is a very common stage when people tend to pass the buck to simply look away and not be Accountable.*

"Not my job" is a standard answer when people are confronted upon why they did not take any action. This is a common excuse, and it has been used in countless discussions to excuse inaction, to redirect blame, and to avoid responsibility. The most common places to find and experience this is in Government offices.

At this stage, there is an awareness about something that needs to happen to get the result. However, there is an apparent lack of desire to involve oneself. When educated graduate and post-graduate people apply for a government clerk job, they know this well. People follow this throughout their working life because of two reasons, one there's no reward for going out of the way, and there's no punishment for not taking action. They quietly live in the impression that it is not in their best interest for them to take on this "added" responsibility.

"Not my job" gained popularity primarily in the government jobs since it did not provide any incentive for stepping up. In the private sector job, descriptions set the boundaries across which the worker dared not step out. Performance expectations focused on individuals' ability to "do their jobs" rather than on their ability to contribute to "getting the result". Organisations assumed it was okay for departments to fight for what they needed instead of working for what was best for the company.

This dereliction is not confined to work; if you look around, you will find the same being deployed at homes as well. The generation of 'Indian boys' raised believed that cooking is not their job. Companies have now started to advertise to promote their brands that say that 'boys' can also do household chores.

46

Now imagine yourself in a large store needing to get some help. You recall the company's slogan that says "we do what it takes to make you happy," you become very disappointed when you only hear, "I'm sorry, but I can't help you, it's technical person's job". Now we can overlook that behaviour in a store but imagine a service person attending a broken down air conditioner telling you this in the peak of summer. The price of such *Stuck Clock* behaviour becomes arduous when you have to pay for it.

Eventually, somebody pays for this 'not my job' behaviour. Sometimes this may not be obvious or visible. It may even be difficult to trace, but ultimately someone pays the price. Perhaps the price will be in how others perceive you; maybe it will be in how the company's performance ultimately affects your pay, maybe it will be in what someone could have done to help you but didn't, because "it's their job." In the end, "Not my job" is a universal excuse that says "don't blame me; it's not my job."

STAGE THREE OF VICTIM CYCLE

3. *It's him: The thirds stage in the Stuck Clock of victim cycle is to look for a scapegoat to pin the blame.*

Let's find someone to blame to cover our *Accountability* is a traditional technique to get rid of the responsibility. This 'game'; is played everywhere, be it workplace or home. However, politicians have perhaps mastered the game. When the ongoing pandemic started to impact the American public, the US Head of the State pinned the blame on China, calling it the Chinese virus. In May of 2020, William Alan Reinsch, Senior Adviser and Scholl Chair in International Business, wrote the following in CSIS (Centre for Strategic & International Studies):

US President has this remarkable ability to change the subject and refocus public attention. This time again, instead of making people think about the administration's fluffy efforts to deal with Covid-19, he has lead by blaming somebody else, well in this case, the whole country, China. He successfully started to debate about how to punish China. Members of Congress of both parties are more than happy to contribute, as they fight among themselves to see who can take the most muscular stance.

For successful buck-passing, one needs to find a suitable victim. Especially if nobody likes them anyway, so, the public can be convinced that they deserve punishment, even if they don't deserve. Here comes the Chinese who fit the bill. Latest Pew Research poll suggests that public sentiment about China has become sharply more negative. There are many factors to this sentiment that are most directly due to the policies of Xi Jinping who presumably has been pursuing to harm the US interests while blaming the virus.

No way am I heading in the direction of the argument that the Chinese don't deserve it.

Whatever be the outcome of the investigation into Wuhan's role in spreading the virus, people won't stop doubting the transparency followed by China. If China had been transparent, precious time might not have lost in saving many lives by finding the vaccine early. Opaqueness is not new to China since they do not allow any international free press or internet services. Any amount of protests from China are not going to make the difference since the world is doubtful about their intentions. Otherwise, what proves their GDP growth while the whole world is reeling under massive GDP downfalls? "It's him" approach is not the solution here too.

Instead of worrying about who did it, the world should be deploying its resources towards finding and distributing the effective vaccine fast to control the damage this pandemic has inflicted.

Regardless of the culprit, this is not the right time to focus on the whodunit. While reeling in the middle of a pandemic, we have to be in it together as a world community. "It's him" can be debated post controlling the pandemic. The present situation demands quick resource deployment to prevent the pandemic and help those who cannot control themselves.

Rather than wasting time on options punishing China, we should be focussing on the possibilities in front of the world to curtail the pandemic. The US, for example, has mulled options ranging from cancelling China's debt, suing China for the damages, imposing more tariffs. We all know that knee jerk reactions to address a problem doesn't work. 9/11 strikes in New York and post display of US might never remove the threat of terrorism from the face of the earth. However, this does not mean to give a free license to China. They surely need to be punished but with valid proofs and ensuring that the basic tenants of their policies take a hit. Chest thumping approach may not be suitable. The whole world is watching that even in the pandemic Chinese continued their expansionist practice by threatening all its neighbours with skirmishes. We must together deal with the situation with the right priorities to avoid a getting into the position of "operation successful, but the patient died".

One can only hope for the sanity to prevail, and any proposed actions against China are not counterproductive. What is profoundly sad about this episode, however, is that rather than the Gandhi's or Mandela's approach of non-violence, the options on the table are muscular threats. As a society, we must move above the blame game and find a way that solves our problems.

There are many pieces of evidence here on how the blame game gets played, "it's him" is not only played at an individual or company level, but it can expand across countries and continents. The blame game can never shift you to *Working Clock* approach. Research shows that when we blame others for their mistakes, we lose self-worth, learn less, and our performance drops compared to those who own up to their mistakes. It also shows that the same logic applies to companies as well. Companies or societies with a widespread blame culture, have a severe disadvantage when it comes to creativity, learning, innovation, and productive risk-taking. The same is visible in India's neighbouring country. That's why creating a culture of psychological safety is one of the most important things a leader should do.

STAGE FOUR OF VICTIM CYCLE

4. *Helpless: The fourth stage in the Stuck Clock of victim cycle is being Helpless. Coming across as having no idea on what to do.*

Confusion / *tell me what to do* was an era in time when managers during the industrial revolution, settled on a management style that involved relating to their employees that they called "Park your brain outside."

These employees could have been very successful at home. They could be the presidents of Residents Welfare Associations, take part in social debates with local political leaders, leaders of local religious bodies handling large amounts of donations. Still, their managers felt that they do not require their skills at the workplace.

I remember about twenty years ago; I used to see many workers used to stand in the local bus queue, with their lunch boxes and office bags, waiting to board the same bus that arrives at a particular time, reach office at a specific time.

Come back home on the same timing bus with an empty lunch box and the housewives would be ready to welcome them day after day with a cup of tea. Initially, I used to wonder how so many people can follow the same routine day after day.

Later in my professional career, I understood the reason for that mechanical life. They are expected to come to work on-time, do routine things, leave on-time, and continue doing so till they retire. Even the retirement functions had a protocol, who to call, who would say what, how many marigold flower garlands (depending upon the retiree position), and how many snacks and sweets would be served. So, everything was "set", no need to apply brains or go out of the line.

Command and Control cultures of the past provided an authoritarian approach to employee involvement - "you just do what you are told, do it well, and we will take care of you for the rest of your life". Some people still depict their organisations as places where you begin work in the morning by "checking your brain at the front door." However, most organisations today run away from this "tell me what to do" culture. This culture creates an environment that attracts, develops, and retains the best and the brightest people. As *Accountability* deepens and people move like *Working Clock* within the organisation, a shift occurs from "tell me what to do," to "here is what I am going to do, what do you think?"- a genuinely insightful and enabling approach to getting results.

Today, some Gen Y and most Gen Z employees expect not only knowing what you want them to do; but also knowing why you want them to do it. This expectation puts additional pressure on today's managers to become "servant leaders," a phrase coined by Robert K Greenleaf. It means the change in leadership style to the needs of your employees.

These modern-day employees are unlikely to leave their aptitude outside and rather be vocal about their opinions even if their leaders never encourage them for their views.

We all know that #1 reason employees leave companies is due to their boss or manager and not because of the company overall. This knowledge means that today's leaders have to provide their team members with the feedback objectively.

If leaders want to retain their best and high potential talent, they should regularly hustle and welcome recommendations, suggestions, and input about company processes from their teams. "*Any company trying to compete must figure out a way to engage the mind of every employee,*" Jack Welch of GE once said.

A few years ago, while working at a mid-management level in a large media company, I was asked by the manager *to do as I say*, and it was not a great feeling. Compared to my previous manager in the same company nurtured me by saying *I trust you, do the best you can, and give the results.* The two approaches impacted my pay-check to go up by 41% in the earlier four years compared to 5% in later two years before I quit. Hence, I could easily see the difference in the leadership approach and its impact on my performance and my pay-check.

STAGE FIVE OF VICTIM CYCLE

5. *Evade: The stage where people like to evade their responsibility and look for cover.*

Another practical stage of the victim cycle is "Shield yourself." In this stage, people continue to seek the protection that comes from behaving in *Stuck Clock* manner. There are several methods that people use when they evade. These could be documenting everything in writing to sending back-up email messages that can be saved and used as proof that they can't be blamed. These people can approach others to substantiate the sequence of events and the nature of the conversations to build a defence that may be helpful in the future.

If an employee keeps checking with their manager twenty times a day, confirming, "Is this right?" and "Are you with me?" He or she also keeps saying, "I just wanted to keep you in the loop about this; just in case I could be doing it wrong" This scenario takes place in offices, labs, and plants across the globe, every day. But the employees are not stopping by and talking with their managers anymore. They have started to copy (cc-ing) their managers on email to cover themselves, and the leaders or managers are okay with it.

When people get advice "Avoid copying people on messages they don't want or need," the typical response is, "I want him to be in the loop in case something comes back to question me."

And when we talk with managers, they rue, "I wish people would stop covering their tails as I get hundreds of copies of messages every day." We need to find out why employees are sending messages through email to their managers who are not interested?

Maybe it is because many managers could be supervising remotely and they never see their people in days. Many industries have stopped the concept of weekly face to face meetings. It's especially becoming visible during the COVID-10 pandemic when managers are managing their people remotely or virtually. It could well be because managers now manage many more people and remotely, so to develop employee confidence, less time is available for coaching and developing in person. Maybe for some companies, they are bogged down in overly cautious or blaming behaviour, leading to a evade mind-set.

Who would question the waste of leadership time, email bandwidth and wasting managers' time when employees frequently copy their managers? It's an open secret that many managers who receive hundreds of emails daily are not reading those where they copied. They are just wishing their employees would stop sending them so many copies while glancing over them.

A sensible manager would put an end to that behaviour swiftly. This manager would coach the employee to accept increasing *Accountability* and ownership. Even then if some employee continue to stop by to ask "Is this okay?" This manager would respond by prompting "What do you think, how can you make a decision?" This approach would make employees bring up topics for approval only in weekly meetings–not in daily encounters.

Managers, if they want to receive fewer email cc's from employees who report to them, they have to clarify about the authority they have. Managers need to coach their employees for accepting their responsibility for their actions and decisions. They have to arrive at an agreement that they will not send you copies of their email except in particular limited circumstances that you agree.

Employees should talk to their managers. Find out what types of emails they want and need to be copied. Develop the knowledge and confidence to stop bringing your manager into the cc loop.

STAGE SIX OF VICTIM CYCLE

6. *Delay / Sleep Over: People remain in the victim cycle, like a Stuck Clock when they avoid taking a decision or procrastinate*

Indian judicial system could be the best example to understand this 'wait and see' approach people take in companies. I have also heard from a very senior corporate leader "not making a decision is also a decision". There are lot of accused individuals in Indian jails, waiting for justice for over 20 years. While, if the case would have progressed at an average speed, they might have walked out acquitted. Many people cannot afford the cost of a legal battle and spend a considerable part of their life languishing in jails. Decades later, the case judgment may have little impact as they would have anyway served the time in prison, waiting for the decision.

"Justice delayed is justice denied" is an old adage. It indicates that legal redressal or relief to the affected party is available. And if that doesn't come in a timely fashion, it is virtually the same as having no remedy at all. For example, the senior management team of a INR 50 bn (US$ 700 mn), beverage products manufacturer and marketer found themselves struggling over the introduction of a new beverage.

Because the company had grown, it lacked clear precedents for such an introduction. After hours of fruitless debate, company officials decided to "wait and see" if the right approach might emerge naturally from the product management group after everyone's emotions cooled down. After months of indecision, a smaller competitor beat them to the punch, making the whole product introduction problem moot. The delaying of the victim cycle often becomes the "sinkhole" of business management as possible solutions get swallowed up in a deluge of inaction.

If the history of most riots that happened in India is studied, one common thing that would appear is the delaying attitude of the decision-makers. Political leaders and law enforcement agencies keep 'sleeping over' the decision to control the rage. This indecisiveness causes irreparable damage to life and property. One of the most talked-about rioting cases of 1984 against a particular community is still awaiting closure after 36 years. The various governments that ruled the nation since 1984 adopted the policy of delay. Only the sufferers of those riots, a lot of widows who lost their husbands and sons can explain the cost of delaying. Sleeping over and waiting for the judiciary to offer a solution has become part of the DNA of Indians. We have reached a stage where people are scared to go to cops and courts, knowing that it's a waste of time and money.

It is not only the Indian judiciary that's a victim of delaying but many more critical functions of the government that are languishing for reforms form decades. India's first women IPS Kiran Bedi and former DGP who took voluntary retirement from police service in 2013, said her mission now is to bring about police reforms. Dr Bedi, at that time, had said she would implement her mission soon. She felt the government's projections to bring police reforms was "just an eyewash". Dr Bedi said the force was used only for the protection of VIPs or other influential people with connections and some threat perception. Therefore, the police had no time for the ordinary people. Perhaps all the energy and resources were deployed to secure the VIPs security but none for the ordinary people. Her motto was that society should not be afraid of the police force. Instead, the police should be a friend of the common man and always be ready to help them," she said.

Alleging that policemen today were being terrorised by the government to settle scores, she said reforms were required to provide respect and dignity to their job and not remain a toy in the hands of the government. Dr Bedi acknowledged that her stint as Director General (DG) of the Bureau of Police Research and Development (BPR&D) facilitated her vision to bring about reforms, something that would not have been possible while working in the government, thus her decision to quit. "At the BPR&D, I could see the government's intentions for police reforms had no program, no vision, and no will to have the reforms; it was merely a deception. Therefore, I thought to have them implemented while remaining outside," she said. Dr Bedi convinced herself that we do not want any more new laws, but only the implementation of the old laws. No point in making new policies daily; instead, the need is in their proper execution. On asking how she planned to achieve her mission, she replied "today is the first day after my VRS request (Voluntary Retirement Scheme) has been accepted... we'll have to *wait and watch*." However, Dr Bedi tendered her resignation from the post of DG of the BPR&D on November 19, 2013, months ahead of her superannuation, and opted for premature voluntary retirement.

She had a run-in with the government when she did not get the post of the Police Commissioner of Delhi. Well, that was her in 2007. After that, she has become part of the same political class that she was so critical. As a governor of a union territory, she has done some excellent work, while running into a frequent tussle with the elected representatives of the union territory. She also contested elections from India's capital New Delhi, for becoming a member of parliament, but could not win. Before that, she was part of the "Anna Movement" with the current Chief Minister of Delhi. However, the Police Reforms remain where they were from ages.

Another very strong need for reforms is in education. India is suffering from an alarming phase of mass-unemployment among degree holder young population. Both post-graduates and graduates are walking pillar to post in search of employment. Just a few days back, there was news that about 6.6 million educated people have become unemployed owing to the COVID pandemic. Many are having graduate and master's degrees and still knocking at the gates of offices, even just for the position of a clerk or an office boy. There's a spurt in suicide cases among the unemployed young men, and unfortunately, the figure is only rising.

Ineffective Education System: The leading cause of this large-scale unemployment among the educated youth in India is our weak system of education. While India is an agriculture-based economy, having more than 60% of the people living in villages and their primary source of livelihood is cultivation.

Unfortunately, a cultivator's son, after receiving a bachelor's degree, does not want to join his father's occupation. He dreams of living a city life and slug it out in cities and towns even if all he gets is a clerical job. Unfortunately, the degrees these youth carry have no relevance to current job requirements. They are exposed to the agriculture methods which are 60-70 years old and do not cover any latest methods of cultivation. They are more than happy to come to cities and take up a junior most job as a call centre executive.

An absence of Cottage Industries: Even with large and predominantly agricultural population, there is a shortage of cottage industries. India needs above everything else, a network of cottage industries which can absorb our millions of unemployed educated youth.

KEY TAKEAWAY

India's educated youth, like any other country, is the pillar of its future destiny. A nation, whose young population struggle in search of a petty clerk's job, cannot make progress in the substantial sense of the term. It is the educated young men and women, on whose shoulder lies the great responsibility of making India a great country. Our young men, on their part, must make it a principle that instead for looking for jobs, they should provide jobs.

However, governments in the last 73 years have failed to make a system for upgrading the education system meeting the evolving industry requirements. While the private sector has come to bridge the gap, but the high cost of education in these institutions makes them unaffordable for the majority of people seeking an education that can link to jobs. An educational system that never gets solved because the government and most of the country's citizens keep waiting to see if somehow, someway a miracle will occur. It won't until Indians get themselves to Working Clock.

GETTING OUT OF THE VICTIM CYCLE

It gives a sense of comfort to people to remain in the victim cycle and thus like *Stuck Clock*. This behaviour often gets amplified in our experience of dealing with government employees versus corporate employees. Typical responses one gets to hear from victim mindset employees are "I don't have to admit I was wrong," "I won't lose face," "I don't have to do anything differently in the future," and "I can justify my lack of performance and growth." Irrespective of the reasons a person likes to remain in the victim cycle, they will never get out of it unless they learn to recognise the attitudes and behaviours that keep them there.

In the absence of such acknowledgement, they will most likely never get the results they want. Let us share the experience of one CEO who learned to spot the traps. Owing to the NDA (non-disclosure agreement) issues, we are changing the names and some situations to share the story. We want to share it with you because it sheds important light on the inner struggles of executives in India today as they attempt to get and stay to the *Working Clock*.

CASE STUDY : THE DILEMMA OF MAYUR VERMA

Mayur Verma was a considerable success in his last assignment as director of new product development, and his performance had left a significant positive mark on the senior management working from different country headquarter. It was almost inevitable that Mayur would rise to be in the senior-most decision-making level at the organisation.

Now to benefit from Mayur's talent and also expose him to production, the top executive committee decided to shift him to production. Towards his career development, his superiors proposed a lateral move to manufacturing where he could bring his talents to modernise the thinking in manufacturing.

Mayur took charge with great expectations and to use his skills to bring a fresh perspective in manufacturing. However, as he approached the end of his first year of managing the production, he was feeling let down at the lack of improvement in its overall performance.

All the Mayur's energy and his out of the box thinking ideas fell flat as there was hardly any improvement in the production issues. Perhaps for the first time in his career, he feared that he might fail in an assignment.

Mayur was not amongst those to ignore and let it continue, even if the performance issue continuing to frustrate him. He decided to engage with the key personnel in the factory to understand what their feeling is. Mayur set up a meeting with Alok, one of the key personnel, over lunch, seeking candid feedback about people's perceptions of Mayur's impact on the factory over the past year. Now that's not something Alok was expecting hence he clarified from Mayur if he wanted to hear the truth.

On Mayur's assurance, Alok opened up and explained how most people attributed a lack of improvement to Mayur's behaviour. Mayur was shocked in getting the feedback like:

"Mayur is too headstrong."

"How can Mayur help, he is not from manufacturing, we need someone who has the manufacturing experience."

"Mayur's intervention has not made any difference at all."

"You can't run manufacturing as you would run new product development".

"Mayur has not been able to do anything for increasing the quality."

"Mayur's communication is not clear."

"Mayur can't take tough decisions."

Mayur was utterly shocked by what Alok shared with him. He couldn't digest what his supervisors think about him. He almost felt aggravated by hearing all the negative feedback. However, he expressed his gratitude to Alok for sharing this with complete honesty. Mayur wondered why manufacturing couldn't accept the blame for its flaws.

The next weekend Mayur went cycling with Mukesh, one of his old friends from new product development. Mayur was meeting Mukesh after a long time after he had left the company to start his own business, soon after Mayur got transferred to manufacturing. However, being old friends, it did not take them long enough to recall the great time they had together in new product development. Mukesh could figure out that Mayur is not in the best of his times and asked him how things were going at the factory.

As Mayur trusted Mukesh, he told him honestly that the situation had turned into a nightmare. Mayur came to a stage where he started venting out to Mukesh. "Mukesh, I've inherited a can of worms. Surprisingly, most people at the factory expect me to do something to solve their problems. I mean, I didn't create their mess! They did. If anyone would have given me the idea about how bad the situation is, perhaps I would have thought over twice to take this position."

"Now, I am stuck. I'm between a devil and deep sea. On one end factory managers deny responsibility, and on the other corporate management expects me to *Fix* the issues. People are quitting factory like its on fire. Morale is low. While I've tried many things, but no one is willing to communicate with others. Everyone blames others for their problems. I think my predecessor would have left seeing that there possibly is no solution to the mess. Here I am supposed to be a superman and solving all the problems myself. There's hardly any way forward suggested by the management committee to the issues I take to them."

Mukesh after hearing all this from his friend Mayur felt a bit surprised. He knew a different Mayur who back then had been supremely confident, a go-to man who thought he could solve any problem which came his way. Now he sounded hopeless, with his reasoning going around in circles. He almost blamed everyone, the corporate management team for putting him in this untenable situation, his manufacturing team for not owning up to their problems. Finally, he blamed himself for getting lost in a set of circumstances over which he felt no power or control.

While Mukesh sympathised with Mayur, deep inside, he knew that continuing to feel victimised is not going to help him move an inch forward to his solution. Mukesh told him "You know, Mayur, I took a coaching course on *Accountability* a few weeks ago, and, based on what I learned there, I'd say you're stuck in what the coach calls the victim cycle. That's the bad news. The good news is that you can do something about it."

As Mayur and Mukesh cycled through Rajpath in New Delhi, Mukesh continued his explanation: "The coach made me acknowledge that everyone falls into the victim cycle from time to time. It's nothing to feel bad. If one can only learn to see when you're falling into it, one can start getting out of it. Victims have no choice but to take control of their future.

The core issue here is *Accountability*, but you can't climb what they called the Steps to *Accountability* without first developing a full understanding of the victim cycle. Think about it. Have you been claiming to be unaware of certain circumstances, pretending not to know what's going on? Denying that it's your responsibility, blaming others. You are attempting to get someone else to take you off the hook. Someone tells you what to do, arguing that you can't do anything, or waiting for things to get better tomorrow?"

These words seemed to strike a nerve in his friend, so Mukesh continued as gently yet forcefully as possible to get Mayur to see himself in a more objective light. "Mayur, I appreciate your professional strength. Remember, it's not that getting stuck in the victim cycle is terrible, it's just not effective. It keeps you from getting results. With this new learning Mayur, now I can see many times when I was in the victim cycle, and that's not bad! The more quickly I can recognise that fact, the faster I can get out of it and start working more productively toward my goals.

Remember the primary issue doctors face is the correct and timely diagnosis and not the treatment of the disease. I know the problems you are facing in the factory are real. I have seen them myself. But with those problems in place, ask yourself what else you can do to rise above those circumstances and get what you want. When you described your situation, I didn't hear many words expressing ownership on your part for what's happened over the past year. You talk as if the manufacturing managers aren't your managers, and as if the factory's problems are something you inherited, that you had no choice in the matter".

Mayur thought about what Mukesh had said, and the more he thought about it, the madder he got. "You make it sound like I'm to blame for everybody else's problems. I don't buy that!" When Mukesh remained silent, Mayur took a deep breath, then apologised for his tirade. "I'm sorry. I guess if I were candid with myself, I would have to acknowledge that I haven't brought my best efforts to bear on the situation at the factory. The only fun I have lately is when I think about the good old days in product development. Things went so smoothly then. Improvements were so visible. It all comes back when I review the weekly update report on my old R&D projects. I always call my old friends to congratulate them and give them advice."

At this point Mukesh interrupted Mayur by saying, "Do you remember in Mahabharata Krishna did not give a choice to Arjun, he told him to do his Dharma. When Arjun hesitated at such a shocking order, Krishna responded, either you are going to fulfil your Dharma or I will, we haven't come this far to go back losing". Mukesh continued by suggesting that it looked to him as if Mayur was looking to escape the battlefield somehow like Arjun wanted, and thus had never completely committed to winning this battle. When he asked Mayur if that were the case, Mukesh confided, that's the case.

He'd hinted to his superiors that he might like to move back to R&D, and he had even interviewed for a job with a competitor. Now, however, he could see that he had been operating lately with one eye on the exit, and had to admit that his situation demanded that he keep both eyes on the problem at hand. Finally, he was able to see that he was stuck in an unproductive cycle playing the victim. And that there were things he could do to improve conditions at the factory if he chose to focus his full attention on the problem.

Specifically, Mayur came to realise that he needed to create a more cohesive team with his managers before any meaningful change could occur. Regretfully, he had done little over the past year to foster a team spirit between himself and the managers who reported to him. Instead, he had simply gone around the managers to the supervisors, meeting with them in early morning meetings to get their input and to give them direction. Mayur acknowledged that he had essentially skirted his managers, and, in effect, disempowered them as a management team.

Strangely enough, Mayur's recognition of his *Accountability* for the factory's poor performance no longer made him feel angry or depressed but increasingly exhilarated. Wanting to feed the feeling, Mayur told Mukesh, "You know, I have been getting in my way and waiting for someone else to solve these problems. While it's true there are a lot of things that have happened to the factory that I had nothing to do with; I've allowed those things to distract me from focusing on the positive action I can take. And, worst of all, my acting like a victim has permitted everyone else to do the same. Thinking about it now, I can even see that a lot of people at the factory are stuck in this cycle, ignoring problems, denying responsibilities, and blaming others. And, as for me, I think I have let myself become so paralysed by the fact that even if I start acting differently, even if I start accepting full *Accountability* for the factory's performance, I could still fail. That scares me."

KEY TAKEAWAY

It's okay to fall into the victim cycle from time to time because it's only human to do so, it's also okay to feel a little scared of the possibility of failure. But the accountable person learns to overcome that fear by recognising that success can only come from getting to Working Clock and working hard to get better results. Sometimes we must be willing to burn our other ships and grasp the helm of the one under our command. Doing so, we can stimulate the conviction and create the ownership necessary to get started on a new program of action and determination to help us rise above our circumstances. With this realisation, Mayur could see that Mukesh was showing him a similar path that Krishna showed to Arjun when Arjun felt incapable of taking action on the battlefield. We never know who can come into our lives to be a Krishna and show us the way. We can only identify Krishna if we are open to acknowledging that we could be wrong, and it's okay to be. But we also realised that we have to take action ourselves, Krishna can only guide us.

FUNDAMENTAL LESSON: SENSING VICTIM FEELING

Like Mayur, there could be countless people' living' every day in the victim mind-set. Even Mayur stayed as a 'victim' for good 12 months before realising that he has to 'do something' about it. That's the first requirement of coming out of victim cycle – acknowledge that you have felt into the victim cycle. This acknowledgement makes you appreciate the high cost you are incurring to stay like *Stuck Clock*. This stage makes you rich with *Observe* perspective that you need to move to *Working Clock*.

Before we move to *Observe* on the Sufferer mind-set, lets us do a small exercise of Yes/No through ten statements below that will tell you if you have a victim mentality. Answer the following questions, either "yes" or "no," depending on whether the scenario in a given question has ever happened to you. As you read each question, be sure to ask yourself "Has this ever happened to me?" or "Have I ever felt this way?" Try to play your own best friend, answering the questions below:

S.No.	Statement	Choice
1	**You Do Not Take Action or Give Up** You will look for any possible reason as to why it's not going to work out, start making excuses, and giving up before you get started.	Yes / No
2	**You Lack Self-Confidence and Self-Belief** You stop believing in yourself that prevents you from following through on your ideas. You start procrastinating, justify excuses, stop taking responsibility and look for escape routes.	Yes / No
3	**You Let Others Take Control Over Your Life** You let others tell you how to live your life since you feel that they know more than you. By following others, you do not take control of your own life. If you put your life in the hands of others, you have no control over your life. You do not take responsibility for your actions and blame others when things go wrong.	Yes / No
4	**You allow the Negative Self-Beliefs Sabotage Your Choices in Life** You give up as per your internal critique. You are okay to settle for things in life which support how you see yourself, not feeling good enough.	Yes / No
5	**You Deplete Yourself Until You Need Support** You run around trying to please everyone — to detriment yourself — until you hit a crisis and need to be rescued. You stop functioning for yourself when you are running on empty. Then, it is everyone else's fault because you carried them and forgot to think about yourself. Then, you can blame them for not meeting your needs when you didn't meet your own needs.	Yes / No

6	**You Feel Bitter and Resentful That You're Not Living Your Life**	Yes / No
	You end up meeting the needs of others because you fear being alone. You give to everyone else, but you are not there for yourself. You don't focus on yourself but instead on living everyone else's life, rather than living your own. When your life falls apart, you end up bitter and resentful at life, not feeling in control.	
	You feel good when pleasing everyone else, rather than focusing on yourself. You rely on your happiness coming from others, rather than fulfilling yourself. You can feel like a martyr, but you're not there for yourself.	
7	**You have an excuses list for Why You Give Up**	Yes / No
	You use excuses list to justify why things will not work out, spoiling your chances to go for what you want and jeopardise your success.	
	You end up escaping being judged, the fear of rejection, or avoiding failure. You avoid your sentiments of not being good enough but end up feeling trash when you give up and never reach where you want to go in life.	
8	**You Engage in Self-Destructive Coping Behaviour**	Yes / No
	You seek instant relief when you're not feeling good about yourself, so you attempt to feel better by engaging in addictions, affairs, or other self-defeating behaviours.	
	You end up damaging yourself and spoiling your life by running away from these unwanted feelings.	
9	**You Beat Yourself Up or Self-Punish**	Yes / No
	You attack yourself with self-blame, punish yourself and berate yourself when things go wrong, when you feel like a victim by self-sabotage and ruining your life.	
10	**It Is Always Someone Else's Fault**	Yes / No
	Being a victim, you blame everyone else because you lack self-responsibility and blame others for things that go wrong	

EXERCISE RESULTS – WHAT THEY MEAN FOR YOU?

Once you have completed the Victim Cycle Self-examination, add up your scores. Give one point for every "Yes" response and Zero points for every "No" response. After adding up your points, compare your total to the scoring table that follows:

If you scored "0" points: You may not have been forthright with yourself.

You should go back and try it again, but this time sit in isolation so that no one can see your results.

If you scored "1" point: You know you are capable of failing like *Stuck Clock*, however, probably you do so more frequently than you're admitting.

If you scored "2-4" points: You can take some pleasure from the fact that we are only human.

If you scored "5-7" points: You know that you can quickly fail like *Stuck Clock*.

If you scored "8-10" points: You have been very honest, absolutely normal, and should be looking forward to what lies ahead in this book journey!

As a normal human being, you may be tempted almost any time to avoid *Accountability*. Like a victim; for the false security and imagined safety of the victim cycle; thus your actual score matters less than that recognition, where it's always someone else's fault that you're not getting results. The recognition that you can fail like *Stuck Clock* sets the stage for you to rise above your circumstances and achieve the results you desire.

You live like a victim because nothing goes the way you want.

The reality could be that you blame everything in life, or everyone, or situations for things that went wrong, rather than looking at how you run away to from the feeling of not being good enough.

If you continue to ignore your internal-self, you are likely to continue to self-inflict, until you deal with the critical part of you. You may be heading to ruining your life with the victim mentality if you let these thoughts take over and affect you.

Having failed to recognise the initial signs of victim mentality, you can be destroying your life. You may not allow yourself to enjoy the good things in life, analyse wrong things in your life, and always see the glass half empty. When you live as a victim, you start to blame everyone, you become an expert in finding excuses, and you begin to blame life or circumstances for things that go wrong. You end up showing self-responsibility and lose control of your life when your inner self-critic takes over you.

This feeling highly impairs your ability to *Observe*; you may need some "Mukesh" to walk-in and help you see it.

MOVING OUT OF THE VICTIM CYCLE

All along in this chapter, you have seen examples of *Stuck Clock* attitudes and behaviour that would have helped you see the difference between being a victim and being Accountable. However, just as Arjun discovered on the battlefield of Kurukshetra, you will have to work hard, get over your fears, understanding Dharma, to spot victimisation attitudes and behaviour in your own life, and the operations of your organisation. In the coming chapters, you'll begin to see *Accountability* with a whole new perspective as you prepare yourself to move towards the steps to greater *Accountability* in your workplace.

CHAPTER

3

Expanding Circle of Influence

There can't be a better story than Mahabharata, to appreciate how influencing changes the future life track. Kauravas had the influence of Shakuni uncle on them, an influence which led them to hatred and war, an influence which made them who they weren't. Whereas Pandavas had with them, the influence of Krishna, the influence that guided them to victory. Thus, we need to choose the right influence in life if we wish to succeed.

Let's look at a modern-day corporate story that played out in India a few years ago. If we recreate the Mahabharata story today, the choice for a parallel character in the world of business to that of the Arjun would be apparent.

CASE STUDY : NESTLÉ INDIA STORY

Nestlé India resurrected itself out of a steep fall inside a pit of fire — like Arjun. The company touched its lows in 2015, with rumours floating that it might shut down. Nestle India, the food and beverages major, emerged as one of the most aggressive players in the FMCG sector by 2018. During the year, it grew its bottom line by 39 per cent while improving the operating profit margin by 400 basis points.

Traditionally Nestlé is considered a slow mover among its peers when it comes to stepping into new areas and venturing into new segments; the company launched more than a dozen products during 2018 while making its presence felt in new categories such as breakfast cereals and pet food. This newly acquired vigour is evident in the fact that new products (over 50 launches between 2016 and 2018) now contribute over a fifth of its growth.

The professional analysis, speed, efficiency, and best-in-class roll-out of new products on POS (point of sales) and online platforms displayed by Nestlé India in 2018 were unmatched. Further, consumer sampling and engagement activities ensured availability, visibility, and accessibility of its brands and products. The firm tapped fast-growing shopper and consumer opportunities on the e-commerce channel.

Nestlé India used this low period to augment its execution skills, distribution base and sales to secure the leadership position in most categories. However, the story is incomplete without a mention of its flagship offering, Maggi noodles. The company took the controversy related to Maggi noodles, head-on. The firm, battered by rumours of the presence of harmful elements in Maggi in 2015, opened the doors of its manufacturing units to consumers. In a series of videos, it showcased the entire Maggi noodles manufacturing process — from farm to fork. This was done for the first time since the introduction of Maggi Noodles in the Indian market 35 years ago. This was a make or break situation for the company.

"At Nestlé India we would like people to know, the purpose we stand for, which is to enable healthy and productive lives for our consumers," said Suresh Narayanan, Chairman and Managing Director of the company.

The positive shift in Nestlé India's attitude was visible to all. During the crisis, the company's communication machinery maintained a stoic silence. Media and consumers were all looking for clarity, but the absence of it fuelled the rumour mills like a wildfire. State by State in the country started banning the product aggravating the negative environment further that put the doubt on the revival of a 100+ year old entity.

The situation was of Arjun, putting his bow and arrow on the ground, telling Krishna that he won't be able to fight against his own. However, in the case of Nestlé India, the Krishna was sent from the Philippines. Suresh Narayanan, a Nestlé veteran, was brought, by its Swiss parent, a couple of months later gave a new lifeline. Suresh was flown in from the Philippines to take charge of the breaking chariot.

Suresh's crisis management record, in turmoil-hit Egypt a few years ago had probably made him the best candidate coupled with his Indian market experience. Sooner than later, the firm's attitude in dealing with the crisis — and even the harsh business environment in general —became visible, after Suresh's entry into his home turf.

In Suresh's own words, it was crucial to gather courage at the time, as the crisis was taking a tremendous toll on the confidence of the company's 7,000-odd employees. "Every crisis is an opportunity for a company to recommit itself to its values and its purpose. For us, respect, dignity, transparency, and trust are extremely important. We are a company that never takes our achievements for granted, and strives to do better," he said. Suresh, however, does not vie for accepting any credit. According to him, it is the work of Nestlé India's team, the power of the Maggi brand, and consumers' love for it that brought it back to leadership position once again by 2017.

Suresh and his team's hard work paid off. By 2018, the India unit of the world's largest FMCG company by revenue became the fastest-growing business unit. Nestlé India was featured among the top 15 subsidiaries of Nestlé SA.

"The Nestlé India we are building is for the next 100 years. The actions of the last few years have certainly set the tone for the next few decades," quoted Suresh Narayanan.

People like Suresh Narayanan know fully well the pitfalls of victim attitude and how to move towards *Working Clock* by demonstrating their influence in not only the immediate team but the whole organisation.

DEFINITION OF *ACCOUNTABILITY* IN DICTIONARY

Unfortunately, however we feel that on the road to results, our society has adopted a much too shallow definition of *Accountability*, one that is myopic in scope and that, ultimately, does not create the empowering influence of true *Accountability* – that is the point of this chapter.

Dictionary.com defines *Accountability* as:

Accountability is the obligation to explain, justify, and take responsibility for one's actions.

Accountability is the state of being accountable, meaning responsible for something or obligated to answer to someone, such as a person with more authority, like a boss.

If you read carefully, is this the real definition of *Accountability*? Is this definition promoting a somewhat negative view of *Accountability*? Notice "*Accountability* is the state of being accountable, meaning responsible for something or obligated to answer to someone, such as a person with more authority, like a boss" implying, that *Accountability* is a state someone creates for someone else.

Media, business definitions, and societal norms reveal that most people understand *Accountability* as something that happens to them or is inflicted upon them, choosing to perceive it as a heavy burden to carry.

For a lot of people, *Accountability* is like a concept or principle that needs to be used when things go bad. Or when someone else is trying to find out the cause and pinpoint blame. Often, when traffic is smooth, and failure has not yet sunk the roads, people rarely ask "Who is accountable for this or that?" It seems that only when the monsoon rains lash Indian cities, do people start looking around for the responsible party. While it is an annual exercise and after every heavy downpour, one gets to witness the dance of pointing fingers on each other.

Majority of us would be looking at the definition of *Accountability* as provided by Dictionary.com as gospel truth. Hence, no surprises they spend so much time explaining and justifying poor situations and finger-pointing on others.

In Nestle India's Suresh Narayanan's case, we honour his approach to *Accountability*, instead of looking for a fall guy, he plunged into the situation and turned it around. Nevertheless, upon encountering a less than the hoped-for result, most people begin preparing their explanations, citing such tired excuses as "we were over budget, overextended, overloaded, under-informed, underfunded, and underutilised." As a result, millions of people in thousands of organisations continue to invest their hard-earned time and waste energy by justifying their lack of performance instead of focusing on ways to improve performance.

QUICK REFERENCE – EXCUSE LIST

As excuses are the obvious response to lack of *Accountability*, let us make it simple for those who use them often, they can just say a number to convey their option:

1. *"We've always done it this way."*
2. *"I thought somebody else would do it."*
3. *"You never said you needed it right away."*
4. *"I didn't know what time you wanted it."*
5. *"It is not done in our department."*
6. *"I expected somebody would tell me what to do."*
7. *"I kept waiting for the go-ahead."*
8. *"Nobody told me not to do that."*
9. *"How do I know, I was told to do it this way."*
10. *"I never know."*
11. *"It slipped my mind."*
12. *"You never said it was that important; I would have done it."*
13. *"I have so much to do."*
14. *"I was ill-advised to do the wrong thing."*
15. *"I assumed that I had informed you."*
16. *"You should have asked me?"*
17. *"I wasn't invited to the meeting - I didn't get the email."*
18. *"My team messed it up."*
19. *"I thought it's not that critical, nobody checked with me."*
20. *"I relied upon someone to do it."*

The list above may sound familiar, well that's the way it is. People in their daily life become so much used to using one or the other reason above that they never realise when it becomes a part of their behaviour. If people like to come out of that behaviour, they need to come to the definition of *Accountability* they followed for so many years, i.e. *Accountability* is a state someone creates for someone else.

Almost every time, whenever something goes wrong in an organisation, professional, or government, people often start playing the "blame game". They immediately begin searching for someone inside or outside the group responsible for the failure. One can see such games being played almost daily while reading the newspaper. Consider all four seasons in the Indian capital. Any onslaught of a new season comes with its own list of known blame games.

If it rains heavily, state and central agencies point fingers at each other for whose job was it to *Fix* the drainage problem or it's because of Metro construction, it rained above normal this year, we didn't have budgets because of the Covid-19 situation, half of our workers were in quarantine, and the list goes on. The list of excuses start to roll out as the pollution level increases beyond "severe category" then we will roll-out an odd-even scheme for vehicles, but it comes with the exemption of most polluting vehicles i.e two-wheelers.

Talking of Delhi, it had a target to install 100 pollution towers at main locations, so far in the last ten years, Delhi has seen only two towers. We will prepone or postpone the school term. We expect private companies to stagger their working times to reduce traffic-related pollution. Come summers and the power outages begin, in fact nowadays it has become a routine feature in winters too. The local government starts to threaten the power distribution company for penalties while giving all types of subsidies to people for cheap power. So, if you see in these examples, too often, the blame game excludes any intention of rectifying the situation.

People dive for the shelter of excuses, explanations, justifications, and disassociations to make sure the spotlight shifts to someone else. Decades of apathy by governments and public authorities have made us so used to oblivion to the price one pays for such abdication of responsibility.

CASE STUDY : INDIA'S FOUR WORST MAN-MADE DISASTERS

Let us look at the four worst man-made disasters India faced owing to someone passing the buck.

It is appalling to see that the responsible authorities seem to sleep over tragedy after tragedy and learn nothing from them, and life just seems to move on. There's little concern or value for human life. Government bashing is easy, but we also need to share some blame. We allow the government to carry on with little *Accountability*. We do not question those in power at the bureaucratic, political, or private business level. We must question *Accountability* frequently. These are the four worst man-made disasters in India linked to gaps in *Accountability Fix*ing.

BHOPAL GAS TRAGEDY OF 1984

It was a spine chilling experience for all those present on the night of December 2-3 1984 in Bhopal, Madhya Pradesh, India. The night of December 2, toxic Methyl Isocyanate (MIC) gas leaked from the factory owned by Union Carbide of India. The entire densely populated area around the factory was engulfed in the deadly gas. When people got up in the morning, they couldn't breathe. When they ran outside their homes to breathe, they ended up taking in more of the deadly gas. Scores went blind, and many never got up from their sleep. Several people suffered from post-trauma diseases over a period of time. Many are suffering even today. With about ten thousand deaths, this remains one of the worst chemical disasters globally, while the actual number of fatalities remains disputed even today. Over half a million people are still fretting with injuries. Poor supervision, coupled with human error, resulted in the tragedy. Unfortunately, no lessons learnt, and even today, several industries in India continue to operate with very little government pressure on them to adhere to safety norms.

HOSPITAL FIRE AT AMRI, KOLKATA

Early morning of December 9, 2011, in Kolkata a fire broke out in the basement of AMRI Hospital. Around 3 am when most patients and attending staff were asleep; they got trapped in the fire. The fire spread rapidly to higher floors. People got trapped inside wards and with no exit possible. All windows had grills. The rapid spread of the deadly smoke proved to be more harmful than the fire itself. Staff's protocol stopped them in reacting quickly and calling for fire department immediately as the fire broke. Slum-dwellers from the nearby area were the first responders at the site. They were the first ones to take up the initiative of rescuing the patients. They broke windows and grills to access the hospital to gain entry inside the hospital. A total of 160 people were inside the hospital at that time. , 89 of them lost their lives, with 85 patients and four staff. Well known callousness to implement most of the mandatory fire safety norms, as laid down by the authorities resulted in the loss of lives. Adding to this was a lack of clear Standard Operating Procedures for such emergencies.

GIRISH PARK KOLKATA FLYOVER COLLAPSE

The most recent man-made disaster occurred in March 2020, at 12.25 pm when a portion of the under-construction Vivekananda Road flyover at Girish Park crossing collapsed, crushing 18 people to death and leaving over 78 injured. Construction work on the 2.2-kilometre flyover was going on since 2009. Like any other government projects, it also missed several deadlines. The assigned builder IVRCL had been pressing the West Bengal government to release funds owing to project cost that had escalated significantly over the years and, which has not been forthcoming. IVRCL had been under pressure from the state government to complete the project, with an eye on forthcoming elections.

While delays in completing the project were mainly on account of several land acquisition litigations that the government had to settle, some politically motivated. Who knows if key stakeholders set aside caution and technical logic in trying to complete the project fast? It may still be early to conclude whether the poor construction or material contributed to the tragedy. However, it is clear that the lack of supervision by the authorities led the contractor to be lax on quality monitoring as construction progressed.

LALITA PARK, DELHI BUILDING COLLAPSE

On November 15 2010, a five-story residential building in a crowded neighbourhood of Lalita Park in East Delhi collapsed like a pack of cards. Eighty injured and 66 lives lost in the incident. Floods in the city, poor quality of construction, or illegal addition of floors could be the cause of the collapse. But once again, the incident highlighted official apathy towards illegal construction and poor monitoring of existing buildings that pose a threat.

Historically, Maha Kumbh Mela stampedes caused by poor people management and lack of adequate infrastructure to monitor and manage large crowd gatherings has been a bane in India, with few lessons learned. One of the worst such incidents took place February 3, 1954, on the occasion of Maha Kumbh Mela in Allahabad, Uttar Pradesh. The ensuing stampede took away 820 lives and left 100 people injured. Such incidents are not uncommon; a similar incident occurred at Mandher Devi temple in Wai, district Satara in Maharashtra on January 26, 2005. The stampede led to 350 lives lost and leaving over 200 injuries. Perhaps all the authorities across states only wake up after the deadly accidents occur. They jostle to safeguard themselves and pin the blame on others.

This provides us with another reminder of the painful "cost" being paid with the loss of human lives owing to the abdication of *Accountability* at various levels.

The downward spiral continues, aided by a wrong-headed understanding of *Accountability*, more and more people are learning to be adept at playing the blame game. Day in and day out while the projects in organisations are launched, people begin taking detailed notes about the progress. This is less for documenting the success of the project but more to justify the lack of results, just in case if anything goes wrong. People waste so much time and energy to device the mechanisms and processes to save their back and to pin the blame.

Simultaneously, the crafting of the blame game story takes precedence over *Accountability*. Unfortunately, Indians have learned that they live in a society that loves to place blame and *Fix Accountability* on someone so someone else can pay dearly for any mistakes. In such a society, the focus is always on covering your back instead of rising and taking *Accountability*.

By following the *Accountability* definition, according to Dictionary.com, we are only delaying to comprehend a reactive perspective of *Accountability*. The definition that's focussed on the past while conveniently ignorant of the future. We need to drop the portion " ...meaning responsible for something or obligated to answer to someone, such as a person with more authority, like a boss". People are robbing themselves of the power of *Accountability* - a power that Mahabharata epic defines as the key to a successful future by following Dharma.

RUMMAGING THE DEFINITION OF *ACCOUNTABILITY*

Chalta hai (it's okay) attitude has made us numb to the perils of adjudicating *Accountability*. It is not unusual for people to justify its okay. As a society somewhere, we feed that attitude. As parents support their children by blaming quality of teacher's if they get low grades. People allow people to intrude into reserved compartments of trains to occupy the seats. People accept sub-standard quality goods with the notion that higher quality is always expensive. People use name dropping as a technique to get rid of the punishment for a rule break. People feed their children the destiny of misery and support victims of circumstances behaviours. People are okay to let others break the queues for one or the other reason. People are okay to ride two-wheelers without helmets, jeopardising their safety.

People are okay to hitch a ride in public transport even if it is dangerous as it breaks the rule of maximum allowed capacity. People are okay to support any violation of the law, instead of opposing it. The fact is, whether you are a victim or a pseudo-victim, you will never overcome an excuse mentality related to your hurtful past until you develop a present and future-oriented view of your *Accountability* for getting more out of life. To achieve that shift in how to view things, you must start with a better, more proactive definition of *Accountability*.

The *Dharma's* definition from Mahabharata for *Accountability* can, we believe, help revitalise the Indian character, strengthen the global competitiveness of Indian corporations, improve the quality of products and services produced by companies worldwide, increase the responsiveness of organisations to the needs and wants of customers and constituents, reduce blame game in the world, and expand the happiness, fulfilment, and power of individuals.

If we dissect the word Account-ability, what we get is a combination of Accounting with Ability. The very meaning of Accounting is recording transactions after-the-fact. It is the process that records the transactions once they have occurred.

Instead of proactive *Accountability*, which stresses what you can do now to get better results, the contemporary definition impels people to "account for" what they have done in the past, instead of defining what they will do now and in the future. It should, therefore come as no surprise that the real value and benefit of *Accountability* stems from a person's or an organisation's ability to influence events and outcomes before they happen.

The traditional definition of *Accountability* overlooks the fact that people gain more from an approach than from a reactive one. Additionally, only a complete definition of *Accountability*, one that captures all the historical as well as the current and future aspects of a person's responsibility and one that stresses the proactive instead of reactive, can address India's depleting character and revitalise its institutions. It has to relearn from *Dharma* about *Accountability*. When Arjun gives up his *Dharma* to fight the opponents, Krishna reminds him of his *Dharma* as a warrior. Krishna clarifies the true meaning of *Dharma* that embodies, action-Karma, and consciousness, inner soul leading to *Dharma*-righteousness.

We have constantly been amazed at how local government officials determine when the drains should be desilted in Delhi and potholes be *Fix*ed in Mumbai. In the month of July 2020, a person died in a deluge that occurred out of the first monsoon rain in the Indian capital. The first reaction from the government agency was that people should avoid going through the areas that gets waterlogged every year. Later, the kin of the deceased was given a million rupees (US$ 13500) as ex-gratia.

A leading national news daily reports "Potholes lead to 522 road accidents across the state in 2018 and killed 166 people, an analysis of mishaps by the State Highway Police has revealed." Now if we look at the main cities of the country i.e. Mumbai and Delhi, the administrative response or action is always after-the-fact. Fully aware that it's an annual problem. In Mumbai, the local corporation BMC, the richest city corporation in the country, actually spends one-third of the allocated budget to *Fix* roads full of potholes. This clearly shows that the issue is not of money but *Accountability*.

These are sad examples of the price that is paid when looking at circumstances from only a historical perspective. After-the-fact, it's too late to adjust behaviour and avoid the negative consequences that can follow. This is the primary problem with society's commonly accepted view of *Accountability*.

Perhaps it's time we learn the new definition of *Accountability* that includes all the steps from *Working Clock*. Imagine if everyone starts to follow this definition, *Accountability* would become a culture of Dharma in our society:

> *Anyone who Observe, Own, Fix, and Repeat (OOFR)*
> *every action in personal, family, and social life*
> *can be called Accountable.*

This new definition can help you and others do all that is possible and necessary to overcome difficult circumstances and achieve desired results.

JOINT *ACCOUNTABILITY* – MAKING THINGS HAPPEN

Let us look at a classic case of how joint *Accountability* is fought for credit and blame game. There was a time when Delhi became the worst affected city in the country in terms of the number of positive corona cases. The pressure was immense. The people of Delhi were both scared as well as angry as they did not see any material action on the ground by the Delhi government. Instead, they had the painful memories of how migrant labourers were incited to return to their villages in the absence of any employment or shelter. People were confused with the flip-flop statements. Here's the situation explained in 10 points for understanding how joint *Accountability* was set aside.

In June 2020, as the Covid-19 cases rose, the political fight between the Centre and the Delhi government had intensified over how to manage the Covid-19 situation in the city. While Covid-19 was spreading very fast in Delhi, the management of the pandemic has left the 20 million residents of the city perplexed as the Centre, and the Delhi government have been seen engaging in a fight. Here's what unfolded:

1. The Delhi government and union government have always been at loggerheads on how to manage the Covid-19 situation playing out. The differences became sharper when Prime Minister Narendra Modi announced the reopening of the economy with a graded exit from coronavirus lockdown

2. As expected, Delhi Chief Minister Arvind Kejriwal opposed to the union government's classification of red, orange, and green zones and putting the whole of Delhi in the red zone. Kejriwal wanted the early opening of shops on the lines of odd-even policy and limiting the curb to sealed premises only.

3. As the lockdown reopening began, Delhi saw a sudden spike in coronavirus cases. On June 6, 2020, the state government decided to reserve the Delhi's hospitals only for the residents of Delhi. This turned out to be another very controversial decision. Following day, Lieutenant Governor Anil Baijal rescinded that order.

4. LG Baijal is the head of the Delhi Disaster Management Authority (DDMA) that takes the final call on Covid-19 management. Interestingly Delhi government did not raise an objection to Baijal's revoking its order.

5. However, just three days later, state's deputy chief minister Manish Sisodia said Baijal's reversal decision had caused a "big crisis" in Delhi impacting their fight against Covid-19.

6. By June 15, Manish Sisodia said that the Covid-19 situation in Delhi was frightening and the cases could breach 5.5 lakh by July-end - resulting in it becoming the worst-affected city in the world. Interestingly, this change was sudden since only a few days before, CM Kejriwal had said about being "fully prepared now" and staying "four steps ahead of corona".

7. The union government's intervention in Delhi became obvious around mid-June as country's Home Minister, Amit Shah met with LG Baijal and CM Kejriwal, ordered the transfer of four IAS officers to manage the Covid-19 situation in the city, and directed door-to-door survey in the hotspots.

8. A fresh fight erupted around mid-June when LG Baijal issued orders for mandatory institutional quarantine of Covid-19 patients. Kejriwal protested leading to LG Baijal revoking his order.

9. A fresh order issued after that which said that all those found positive for the virus, have to report to a Covid-19 designated Centre. This Centre will decide if they need quarantine, hospitalisation, and institutional quarantine, or monitored home isolation is sufficient.

10. Again, Deputy CM Manish Sisodia had raised objection to this order in his letter to the union home minister, Amit Shah. Sisodia mentioned the logistical issues with inconvenience to

patients. He said that it would be very difficult to transport patients owing to a lack of ambulances and healthcare staff. The patients would have to stand in long queues even when they may be seriously unwell.

Fortunately, with the intervention of the Union Government, the pandemic situation eased a lot. Towards the end of July, the positive caseload in the city was only 133k with about 11k only active cases. Different from what was predicted by the Delhi government that it could well be half a million cases by the end of July 2020.

Here's just one example where the two sides could have taken Joint *Accountability* and worked together to fight the global pandemic. Instead, what the citizens of the Indian capital witnessed was a total blame game on each other and credit taking for small achievements?

An important aspect of *Dharma's* definition of *Accountability* involves the fact that *Accountability* works best when people share ownership of circumstances and results. Like Krishna explained to Arjun on the battlefield that he has to do his *Karma* while following his *Dharma*, thus he is responsible as well as accountable. In the traditional definition of *Accountability*, it leads people to assign "individual responsibility," without acknowledging the shared *Accountability* that so often characterises organisational behaviour and modern life.

It is no surprise, and whenever an individual is identified as the one responsible for poor results, everyone feels relieved now that they're "safe." Like we discussed earlier in the Satyam Computers case, while Raju may have been responsible for the downfall, but it does not absolve his other accomplices who joined him in the fudging of records. Therefore, when an organisation fails to perform, it's a collective failure. Whenever we study any organisation's failure, we must keep in mind that while there could be a prime suspect but the *Accountability* must begin with an acceptance of the notion of "*Joint Accountability*."

ACCOUNTABILITY LESSONS FROM SPORTS

Imagine a hockey team where each player assumes responsibility for covering a player from the opposite team. No hard-and-fast rules prescribe the exact point where one player's area ends, and another begins. Given such overlapping areas of responsibility, getting good results (i.e., covering the entire opposition) becomes a team effort wherein individual *Accountability* shifts according to circumstances, and players are always trained to go for the ball, whenever they can reach it, even when more than one player can do so.

For example, you have probably observed the occasion when a ball is pushed into shallow left-centre field. Immediately, the short-stop, the left fielder, and the centre fielder converge at the same time with none of them completely sure of who should catch the ball. Sometimes, the ball gets snatched because the players run into one another or, thinking it could be anyone's ball, they all wait for the other guy to make the catch uncertain, as to who is going to take responsibility for it, this time. Likewise, the organisational game is a "team sport" where everyone has his or her responsibility, where everyone contributes to the final score, and where *joint Accountability* governs the play.

The Indian cricket team is a great example of "*Joint Accountability*". Where "everyone is working together so that they don't drop the catch; but when it does get dropped, everyone dives for the ball to pick it up." In other weaker teams, "too many players see the ball falling to the ground between players but react by saying 'that was your ball.'" In the IPL (Indian Premier League for Cricket) of 2020 that's being played in UAE due to Covid19 concerns, Faf du Plessis, South African cricketer, has demonstrated many times how *Joint Accountability* produces match winning situations. He has been involved in many catches at the boundary where two players completed a catch to avoid getting outside the boundary.

Focus on common results should be the single-most-important uniting factor that facilitates cooperation and collaboration. History has enough examples to show that some of the greatest collaboration were accomplished by a uniting common purpose. India's wining 1983 world cup cricket as underdogs, India placing the first Mars satellite with the collective team effort of ISRO. These examples tell us that collaboration in each situation can be done that otherwise would not likely have been achieved.

CASE STUDY : MARUTI SUZUKI INDIA

The following story illustrates the power of *joint Accountability*. An Auto industry SME company was readying to dispatch the dashboards of the new car launch for Maruti Suzuki India Ltd. All future business depended upon the on-time delivery of their prototype. All the employees of the company gathered near the dispatch area on a Saturday to celebrate the send-off, the Jaipur Golden Transport driver, who'd been contracted to transport the stock, was greeted with cheers and good wishes. He was surprised to see the emotions and warmth every employee had towards the dispatch.

Middle of the night, somewhere near Manesar, at a highway weighing station, the driver discovered that he was carrying about 200 kg extra load over the permissible limit for his lorry. Now he could neither go back nor forward since this overweight problem, would result in a one-day delay, and the paperwork would require more time with the company. While having tea with his assistant at a roadside Dhaba (eatery), he thought of all the happy faces who were dependent on him while sending him off. So, he asked his assistant to pull out a spade from the toolbox. The assistant was a little sceptical but followed the driver's instructions. The driver with the assistant went to the nearby farm and dug a pit of about 8 x 3 feet. They pulled out the extra tire, rain cover, toolbox, their personal belongings, and other non-essential stuff from the truck and put it in the pit and covered it. Eureka, the weight got reduced by 250 kilograms. The driver was committed to delivery on time; thus, he became a part of the team. The next day he delivered the cargo on time to the Maruti Suzuki plant at Gurugram, Haryana.

Think of it, the driver was not expected to go out of the way, risk his stuff and be accountable but he became jointly accountable for results and to solve problems and overcome obstacles he personally invested in a collaborative process. That's the power of joint *Accountability*—it drives collaboration, cooperation, and cross-boundary solutions.

Specific to the Indian context, let's look at how *Joint Accountability* bore the fruits of labour. It takes a village to raise a child, is an African saying. Ensuring that the child has a textbook in her hand when she grows up requires synchronised actions at multiple levels. Various parts of the government need to work together to make that happen. In any state, delivery of public service is complex. Problems are not limited to a particular school, locality, or government institution. Focus on the myopic isolated service delivery issues is likely to confuse us with the symptoms of *Accountability* breakdowns.

To find a solution, we need to look at *Accountability* differently. Support has to be provided to reformers so that they can forge diverse coalitions. This would help them navigate the complexity to drive the required change. These type of coalitions should be competent to concurrently influencing various levels of government. They should be vertically integrated for monitoring links in the chain of the service delivery involving local, to the state, and even national level.

How a more holistic concept of *Accountability* needs to emerge for public finance is captured in Paolo de Renzo's work on the budget *Accountability* (Paolo de Renzo is Senior Research Fellow at the International Budget Partnership (IBP) in Washington, DC, and an Adjunct Professor at the Institute for International Relations at the Pontifícia Universidade Católica of Rio de Janeiro (PUC-Rio).

93

Forming coalitions for the division of labour that allow each organisation to focus on what they do the best is echoed by Jillian Larsen's research.

CASE STUDY : SAATHI & SAMARTHAN

What does doing *Accountability* differently in India means? Civil Society Organisation (CSO) in India documented two case studies. Samarthan (Samarthan-Centre for Development Support is a leading non-profit organisation working in the Indian states of Madhya Pradesh and Chhattisgarh since 1995) and SATHI (Support for Advocacy and Training to Health Initiatives) provide new insights into how differently applied *Accountability* may look like.

SATHI's work has been going on for decades to improve public healthcare in the western Indian state of Maharashtra. The organisation has worked bottoms up, starting from the village level. They have organised social audits of individual health clinics, mobilising networks of CSOs to help communities investigate and document problems, and propose solutions. SATHI goes beyond audit findings to help improve individual health clinics. They also identify gaps and hurdles at higher levels of government. SATHI has been able to leverage its CSO networks and its official position on government committees. They have pushed for changes wherever they were required — from the village, district, state or national level. SATHI has bridged the gap between those directly affected by problems in the health system and decision-makers and their executors.

SATHI's strategy seems to be working nicely. Their strategy has already resulted in the expansion of cooperative practices in the health sector of Maharashtra. SATHI, with its experience of community-level work, was successful in showing that community-based monitoring is more likely to get positive ratings compared to those that were not. This insight enabled SATHI to leverage its knowledge, experience and networks to influence the local state government to expand this practice to other parts of Maharashtra.

Similar to SATHI, Samarthan has a good track record of addressing governance issues. A support organisation in Madhya Pradesh and Chhattisgarh is addressing the challenges of poverty and underdevelopment through strengthening the grassroots civil society. Improving work under the Mahatma Gandhi National Rural Employment Guarantee Scheme (MGNREGS) is one of its key focus areas. MGNREGS is reportedly the world's largest social security scheme, MGNREGS guarantees 100 days of paid work to every rural household in India.

This endeavour is directed towards public works projects. The local communities identify the priorities per the local situation. The scheme if implemented rightly, can be transformative to millions of poor households in rural India. Like many things, it is impacted by corruption, inefficiency and manipulation at multiple points starting from village level to the state level.

Samarthan was quick to learn that *Accountability* breakdowns flouted simple groups. They discovered that the problem could be ranging from having systemic holes in its administration until a village level implementation. Samarthan decided to become a channel for tackling both ends. They tapped their grassroots networks to coordinate social audits at the village level. Samarthan also organised a training session with the local officials administering the project. While at the same time, they actively engaged with CSO networks, like the People's Budget Initiative, to bring structural issues to the front.

Both SATHI and Samarthan's work has remained deeply connected to the truths of how service implantation happens on the ground. This change has helped local sections and organisations for tackling issues that are specific to a particular block or village. While Samarthan is also able to influence higher levels of government for problems that are broader and more systemic.

SATHI and Samarthan appear to be working in ways that epitomise "*Doing Accountability Differently.*" They have not scaled up by just observing more and more groups or health facilities. Instead, both organisations have gone ahead with a more holistic view of *Accountability*. They joined or created networks allowing them to engage in observing and seeking approval from multiple levels of state machinery. Both of them kept a firm grounding at the village group level while creating the required capacities to steer through the political and technical layers of governments at the state and national levels. They both succeeded to observe indicators, identify the root causes, and develop their participative action plan properly.

Both of these organisations did not only focus on creating the perfect policy solutions while both are well placed to do so. Their objective has not only been having a seat at the table, while both are involved in various official bodies that allow them access. They have been effective in being able to shrewdly steer a complex public service delivery system and assemble powerful networks of reformers to amplify their voice — and the voices of those they serve — so it reaches the ears of those who need to act.

Organisations where the idea of individual responsibility drives the system, an issue will arise, such as product recalls, missed sales targets, or cost overruns. Each of these issues will prompt "other" departments to sit back and rest quietly, relieved that a particular issue lies outside their department's *Accountability* and thankful that they are not the ones on the "critical path." While in the environment of *Joint Accountability*, everyone realises that most issues extend beyond department lines and require solutions that often necessitate cross-department involvement. But how does *Joint Accountability* work, and how do you manage it? How do you avoid getting dragged like a *Stuck Clock* when someone with whom you share *Accountability* gets stuck in the victim cycle? The answers to these questions come from learning to hold other people accountable for the desired outcome as you hold yourself.

CASE STUDY : TIN PLATE MANUFACTURING COMPANY

There are numerous examples in all factories and service corporations where individuals stood up to take up the *Accountability* or a team ensured that the objectives are met on time. While doing a project in one of the largest tin plate manufacturing companies, we heard the following stories from two different sets of people.

In one assembly line, there was a worker in the third shift who would often slip away from the line duty and consume alcohol in the corner of the factory. One of his colleagues observed this behaviour and tried explaining to him the repercussions. However, the worker at fault never paid heed to the advice and continued with that behaviour. The production numbers and quality started to deteriorate, and the supervisor called out the meeting of all workers for that production line. The defaulting worker had no remorse and was acting unaware of the situation. The worker who tried to explain to him in private felt very bad that due to him, the entire team is getting punished. However, he tried once again to talk to the erring colleague and almost threatened him that he would not be able to hold their secret.

Hearing this, the erring worker used the common victim excuse and narrated how he is under tremendous pressure at a personal level. How his family is expecting so much from him, but he has limited means. Hearing this, his colleague sympathised and promised that he will never share this secret with anyone and will try his best to cover him up wherever possible.

Now, the story of another production line. The line reported extra wastage of tin plate being cut from margins. The supervisor called the meeting and told the team that this must be stopped, and they should collectively find the reason. Everybody got together and tried to find the issue. They figured out that the problem was with the spindle alignment on which the heavy tin roll is mounted. They all got together to figure out how they can *Fix* it. The solution came from one of the newer team members who suggested to install an extra steel "arm" arising from the spindle till the end of the roll upwards, to keep the spindle aligned. The team got together and installed the extra "arm" to maintain the alignment. This resulted in reducing the wastage to almost zero.

Now, if we study the above two stories, clearly we see the difference of approach in *Accountability*. While in the first example the *Karma* was at play but perhaps the *Dharma* was missing. The *Dharma* to do the right thing in the right way. In the second example, both *Dharma* and *Karma* played together like a symphony and achieved better results. This is the difference in *Dharma's* definition of *Accountability*.

THE BROKEN SQUARES EXERCISE – *JOINT ACCOUNTABILITY*

The concept of join *Accountability* can also be understood from a widely used training exercise The Broken Squares. The exercise is generally used to drive various learning outcomes like communication, trust, teamwork, time management, and care for each other. However, we realise that it also provides a great learning outcome for *Accountability*. The exercise is done in a group of 20 or more people in groups of five. Each team of five members is given five packets of five random pieces each. The objective is that everyone on the table of five should have five squares of equal size made. The exercise goes on until all the tables complete the task.

It is usually observed that the first person who completes the square formation, sit backs and relaxes, feeling victorious. He also feels frustrated about why others are not able to complete. While he gets frustrated, he enjoys the glory of "achievement". Now, he does not realise that until he breaks his square, others will not be able to complete the square, and the table will never achieve its objective if five equal size squares with everyone. Another behaviour that's observed is that when one table completes the task, they start to celebrate and laugh on others or disturb them while others are struggling to complete. They miss the task brief that the exercise would go on until all tables complete their task. When it's all over, the exercise shows that *Accountability*, in the organisational setting, is not fully achieved until everyone understands that individual *Accountability* includes an appreciation for Joint *Accountability*.

CASE STUDY : 'ROHINI' SATELLITE - LAUNCH STORY

The importance of *Joint Accountability* and ownership is beautifully narrated in the book Wings of Fire by Dr APJ Abdul Kalam, former President of India and ex-chief of ISRO (Indian Space Research Organisation). In his own words:

"In 1973, I became the project director of India's satellite launch vehicle program, commonly called the SLV-3. Our goal was to put India's "Rohini" satellite into orbit by 1980. I was given funds and human resources — but was told clearly that by 1980 we had to launch the satellite into space. Thousands of people worked together in scientific and technical teams towards that goal. By 1979 — I think the month was August — we thought we were ready. As the project director, I went to the control centre for the launch. At four minutes before the satellite launch, the computer began to go through the checklist of items that needed to be checked. One minute later, the computer program put the launch on hold; the display showed that some control components were not in order. My experts — I had four or five of them with me — told me not to worry; they had done their calculations, and there was enough reserve fuel. So I bypassed the computer, switched to manual mode, and launched the rocket. In the first stage, everything worked fine. In the second stage, a problem developed. Instead of the satellite going into orbit, the whole rocket system plunged into the Bay of Bengal. It was a big failure.

That day, the chairman of the Indian Space Research Organization, Prof. Satish Dhawan, had called a press conference. The launch was at 7:00 am, and the press conference — where journalists from around the world were present — was at 7:45 am at ISRO's satellite launch range in Sriharikota [in Andhra Pradesh in southern India]. Prof. Dhawan, the leader of the organisation, conducted the press conference himself. He took responsibility for the failure — he said that the team had worked very hard, but that it needed more technological support. He assured the media that in another year, the team would succeed. Now, I was the project director, and it was my failure, but instead, he took responsibility for the failure as chairman of the organisation.

The next year, in July 1980, we tried again to launch the satellite — and this time we succeeded. The whole nation was jubilant. Again, there was a press conference. Prof. Dhawan called me aside and told me; you conduct the press conference today. I learned a very important lesson that day. **When failure occurred, the leader of the organisation owned that failure. When success came, he gave it to his team.** *"*

While Dr Kalam narrated this story to drive the leadership quality, we can learn how Prof. Dhawan, while taking ownership of the failure assigned the Accountability of relaunch to the team within a year.

JOINT *ACCOUNTABILITY* – THE JOURNEY

Stephen Covey also explained this concept of joint *Accountability* in his best-selling book 7 Habits of HighlyEffective People. He discussed the sequence of individual growth in different stages.

The journey begins from Dependence, where the focus is to blame others and defend themselves. If results are not achieved, it's because of 'you'.

The next stage is Independence, where people start to take responsibility for themselves. Here people start to use 'I am responsible', 'I can do it', 'I can choose'. Yet, they fail to appreciate the next maturity level of Interdependence. Where the focus shifts from I and You to We.

This is the stage where *Joint Accountability* is understood, and each other's strengths are leveraged to produce outstanding results. Most successful working environments utilise the principles of Interdependence with joint ownership.

Even in the Broken Squares Game, people learn, sometimes late, that they can win provided everybody wins. *Joint Accountability* fosters joint responsibility, and that makes the environment very healthy. One can still commit a mistake, but it would not evoke finger-pointing, but helping hands. Such environments drive high-quality output with motivated stakeholders. It leaves no room for excuses. Every action leads to learning and development instead of fear and punishment. People start to become accountable for their actions.

GITA AND *ACCOUNTABILITY*

Let us see what the connection between Gita and *Accountability* is. The Gita's learning was awarded to the skilled and noble Arjun when he became hopeless in the battleground of Kurukshetra, unable to withstand the challenge of having to fight his friends, relatives and teachers. Krishna gave a message through Gita to rescue Arjun despite his paralysed state of mind.

The Gita is in three parts of six chapters each. The first part talks about you - as an individual. You meet hurdles, and they overburden you. Your conduct should be aligned to your purpose of life. That conduct is your duty; it is *Karma* yoga, a path of action.

In the second part, Krishna teaches the *Dharma* to Arjun. Epitomising that even if one is in a deep state of hopelessness, he is bound to follow *Dharma*. He has to get over the excuses, pains, reasoning, and follow his *Dharma*.

In the third part, Arjun realises that he has no choice but to do his *Karma*. If he has to win over the wrong, he has to follow his *Karma*, irrespective of his challenges. In the 45 minute dialogue, Krishna was able to move Arjun from a state of hopelessness to a state of Purposefulness following his *Karma*.

ACCOUNTABILITY GAP

In Part-I, we understood how *Accountability* and Ownership impact businesses both positively and negatively. We understood that if businesses have to grow, not only the people working for the organisation but also those accountable outside need to step up for exceptional results. We saw various examples of how one man made the whole difference in *Accountability* beyond expectation.

In Part II, we will climb the steps of the ladder to *Accountability*, one step at a time so that you understand, internalise, and can apply each step. We will understand how to gather the courage to *Observe* and acknowledge reality; find the heart to *Own* your circumstances, no matter how challenging that may prove to be; gather the wisdom to *Fix* any problem or any obstacle that stands in your way; and exercise the means to make things happen, allowing you to get the results you want *Repeatedly*.

WHAT YOU CAN EXPECT FROM FUTURE CHAPTERS

✓ It takes time, effort, commitment, and resolve, to get onto the Steps to *Accountability* and remain there. However, once you reach there, there's no way you can drift towards *Stuck Clock* or the victim cycle. You are likely to get drifted, quite likely, but you would know that you are drifting and you would know how to stay on course on the *Working Clock*.

✓ Over the last two chapters, we have discussed the scenarios and examples of how people and organisations get stuck in the victim cycle or *Stuck Clock*.

✓ In the next four chapters, we will discuss the steps to move like a *Working Clock*, which would prepare you towards *Accountability*. You will be able to *Observe* the signs of lack of *Accountability* as by now you know how victimisation won't help you. You would be starting to *Own* the non-conducive circumstances, instead of cribbing about them. You would start to find ways to get out of them. You would be able to *Fix* the situations with interdependent and joint *Accountability*

✓ Once you have practised the first three steps, you would become an expert to know how to *Repeat* them to ensure that you do not slip towards the *Stuck Clock*.

✓ Rising above your circumstances to get the results you seek is the empowering principle operating from *Dharma* and *Karma* teachings of Gita.

PART

II

The *Accountability* Clock

CHAPTER

4

Observe

LESSONS FROM MAHABHARATA

It always takes courage to acknowledge or *Observe* the reality of a difficult situation, and even the most intelligent and righteous people can fail to do so. Let's see what made Bhismapitama in Mahabharata epic fail to *Observe* It. Bhishmapitama was considered a very religious and righteous person in Mahabharata. Then why he did not stop Duryodhan? Instead, he kept silent during Draupadi's disrobing. Not only Bhishma but many other court members didn't say anything, including Pandavas, Dhritarashtra, etc. If Dhritarashtra, the blind King would have instructed Bhishma, he would have easily stopped this misdeed. But driven by blind love, Dhritarashtra used his blindness as an excuse and allowed his son Duryodhan to go ahead. All elders could *Observe* what was going on but failed to act.

Let's first get into the context of Sabha Parva (a congregation of court in the palace) where the vastraharan (disrobing) event happened. A player will stand to lose whatever is kept on the stack with every roll of the dice. Yudhishthira after losing himself in the game, at last, put Draupadi on the stack and lost her too. With that, all Pandavas plus Draupadi became Slave / Dasi of Duryodhan. If Yudhishitra has already lost himself, he had also lost the right to put her on the stack; was Draupadi's defence.

Duryodhan & the company were talking about the technicality of the game and Draupadi, Vidura & Vikarna were talking about ethics. In other words, the former were seeing Duryodhan and Yudhishthira as just players and everything else as a commodity.

In contrast, the latter was seeing them as brothers and everything else from the family values prism. When Draupadi posed this question in the assembly to all elders, Bhishma said

"O blessed one, morality is subtle. I, therefore, am unable to duly decide this point that you have put, beholding that on the one hand one that has no wealth cannot stake the wealth belonging to others, while on the other hand wives are always under orders and at the disposal of their lords. Yudhishthira can abandon the whole world full of wealth, but he will never sacrifice morality. The son of Pandu said--'I have won.'

Therefore, I am unable to decide on this matter. Shakuni is not his equal among men at dice-play. The son of Kunti still voluntarily staked with him. The illustrious *Yudhishthira did not himself regard that Shakuni has played with him deceitfully.* Therefore, I cannot decide on this point" Whatever Bhishmapitama said seem to be logical while sounding diplomatic. Ask yourself if you were to decide if Draupadi was won fairly or not. Perhaps the same response of *"Can't say for sure"* will come.

However, one can easily say that the dragging of Draupadi from her room to the assembly and disrobing her was entirely wrong. Such humiliation is not as per *Dharma*, even with the slaves or *Daasi*. Bhishma remained quite due to his oath, but he foresaw the upcoming drama. However, he could not stop Draupadi challenging him to answer as she asked "... Kauravas, I am the wedded wife of King Yudhishthira the just, hailing from the same dynasty to which the King belonged. Tell me now if I am a serving-maid or otherwise. I will cheerfully accept your answer. This mean wretch, this destroyer of the name of the Kurus, is afflicting me hard. Oh Kauravas, I cannot bear it any longer. Oh kings, I desire you to answer whether you regard me as won or unwon. I will accept your verdict whatever it be."

Listening to Draupadi's question, Bhishma answered "I have already said, O blessed one, that the course of morality is subtle. Even the illustrious wise in this world fail to understand it always.

What in this world a strong man calls morality is regarded as such by others, however otherwise it may be; but what a weak man calls morality is scarcely regarded as such even if it be the highest morality. From the importance of the issue involved, from its intricacy and subtlety, I am unable to answer with certitude the question you have asked. However, it is certain that as all the Kurus have become the slaves of covetousness and folly, the destruction of this our race will happen on no distant date. O blessed one, the family into which you have been admitted as a daughter-in-law, is such that those who are born in it, however much they might be afflicted by calamities, never deviate from the paths of virtue and morality. O Princess of Panchala, this conduct of theirs also, viz. that though sunk in distress, you still are easiest the eyes on virtue and morality, is assuredly worthy of them. These persons, Drona, and others, of mature years and conversant with morality, sit heads downwards like men that are dead, with bodies from which life has departed. It seems to me, however, that Yudhishthira is an authority on this question. It behove him to declare whether you are won or not won."

Bhishmapitama's response above demonstrates the fact that no matter how protected we may be in this world if we fail to Observe, we will end up paying a high price. Our learning could be that despite Draupadi having five husbands, all seniors and most intelligent men of the moment present, one can be ravished by failure to Observe. Even while being present in the state assembly, having all Draupadi's five protector husbands around, Lord Krishna had to come and save his sister from a lifelong scar. Krishna, instead of getting into the technicalities of the situation, Observed and concluded that he had to intervene. He looked at the situation from a professional prism. Here's Draupadi who has been put into a situation for which she is not at all responsible. She has failed to make everyone in the assembly to Observe, eventually calls out Krishna to save her.

Krishna makes us learn that we should not let ourselves get blinded and fail to *Observe* It.

Bhishma and other elders did not duck the question, but they refused to *Observe* It and took shelter under technicality vs. ethics. That's where they made a mistake; they failed to *Observe* It because *Dharma* or morality was more on the ethics side than the technicality of the game.

CORPORATE LESSONS

On the corporate front, let's take up the case of Intel Corporation, how they failed to *Observe* It coming and went downward spiral.

CASE STUDY : INTEL STORY

2016 is when Qualcomm started enforcing licensing and purchasing terms so ruthlessly that made it almost impossible for manufacturers to offer Intel-based mobile devices. We wonder what stopped Intel finding a US company to produce a phone around their chip when the original Xolo X900 was well-positioned against a then-current iPhone. Qualcomm inflicted a stranglehold situation on the market behind the scenes, that left Intel way behind.

In the year 2012 Intel's first credible smartphone, Xolo 900. While it wasn't a match for more powerful devices around that time, but it was a great effort. Also, the Medfield SoC chip that powered the Xolo 900 phone was meant to be a foothold, indication for things to come. However, four years and billions of dollars later, it's become clear that Intel had lost the plot for smartphone and tablet market as it cancelled all of its 14 nm tablet SoCs and 14 nm smartphone SoCs that would have shipped in Android devices. The company was diving into 5G research and hoped to lead the industry in developing 5G products.

Intel's attempts to break into the merchant foundry business by attracting a handful of high-margin customers weren't all that successful and couldn't generate required revenue for them. The distinction between IDMs (integrated device manufacturers) and merchant foundries like Intel is the root cause of why Intel's mobile efforts nosedived the way they did. Intel's manufacturing strategy relied upon rapidly adopting new process technology. The bulk of the company's revenue was derived from leading-edge nodes; older facilities were either upgraded or shut down as they became obsolete. Intel's R&D expenses calculated as a percentage of total sales as compared to competition like Samsung and TSMC (Taiwan Semiconductor Manufacturing Company) were very high.

TSMC pursued different optimisation strategies. While it also invested in leading-edge semiconductor technology, the bulk of TSMC's revenue was earned on older technology nodes. Intel made limited use of its older facilities to build its chipsets, but its business model was fundamentally different.

For most of the 30 years, that difference didn't matter. From the 1980s to 2010, Intel could beat its low-volume RISC competitors and seized its strength in economies of scale it created in the PC market for consumers. It defeated its only serious competitor in the x86 market and forced AMD to sell its labs for survival. Intel pushed volumes in new markets by leveraging economies of scale it had created somewhere else.

Intel's failure to gain propulsion in the mobile market highlights the flaws in looking the other way from technological progress as a roadmap for corporate success. Despite delays and its own decision to abandon its tiktok, analogue model, Intel still owned the most technologically advanced foundries in the world.

All of this is true — as is the fact that Intel spent $10 billion on mobile with nothing to show for it. Intel also set out to include the layoff or redeployment of 16,000 employees, according to speculation from one website.

It's astonishing to see such giants as IBM, General Motors, Sears, and US Steel, who at one time were seen as the unchallenged leaders in their respective world markets, suddenly fall because they were not able to *Observe* in time and respond fast enough to the revolutionary changes that occurred in their marketplaces.

CASE STUDY : HOW DARE YOU?

"How dare you?" – Almost became a slogan from a 16-year-old Swedish girl when she roared at the UN climate conference in September 2019. It took a 16-year-old to shake the highest international body to wake up and get real about their *Accountability*. She compromised her entire school year to raise all the noise around for people to start becoming Accountable towards the depleting environment. In September 2019, she travelled to New York to address a UN climate conference. Ms Thunberg didn't fly because of the greenhouse gas emissions from aviation. So her trip from Europe to the United States was by a boat — a racing yacht starting from Plymouth, England, and she arrived in New York harbour to much fanfare in August 2019. She triggered, millions of people around the world taking part in a climate strike, underlining the scale of her influence. Addressing the conference, she blasted politicians for relying on young people for answers to climate change. She said: "*How dare you? I shouldn't be up here. I should be back in school on the other side of the ocean, yet you all come to us young people for hope. How dare you?*"

GRETA THUNBERG: UK PARLIAMENT SPEECH

Before that UN speech that gave her the international platform, she has been raising concern and awareness across Europe. She was the champion in her Swedish school to make school children strike outside the school to convey her message. Back in April 2019, she addressed the UK parliament and here's the transcript to her full speech:

My name is Greta Thunberg. I am 16 years old. I come from Sweden. And I speak on behalf of future generations. I know many of you don't want to listen to us – you say we are just children. But we're only repeating the message of the united climate science. Many of you appear concerned that we are wasting valuable lesson time, but I assure you we will go back to school the moment you start listening to science and give us a future. Is that really too much to ask?

In the year 2030, I will be 26 years old. My little sister Beata will be 23. Just like many of your own children or grandchildren. That is a great age; we have been told. When you have all of your life ahead of you, but I am not so sure it will be that great for us. I was fortunate to be born in a time and place where everyone told us to dream big; I could become whatever I wanted to. I could live wherever I wanted to. People like me had everything we needed and more. Things our grandparents could not even dream of. We had everything we could ever wish for and yet now we may have nothing. Now we probably don't even have a future any more.

Because that future was sold so that a small number of people could make unimaginable amounts of money. It was stolen from us every time you said that the sky was the limit, and that you only live once. You lied to us. You gave us false hope. You told us that the future was something to look forward to. And the saddest thing is that most children are not even aware of the fate that awaits us. We will not understand it until it's too late. And yet we are the lucky ones. Those who will be affected the hardest are already suffering the consequences. But their voices are not heard.

Is my microphone on? Can you hear me?
Around the year 2030, 10 years 252 days and 10 hours away from now, we will be in a position where we set off an irreversible chain reaction beyond human control, that will most likely lead to the end of our civilisation as we know it. That is unless, in that time, permanent and unprecedented changes in all aspects of society have taken place, including a reduction of CO_2 emissions by at least 50%.

And please note that these calculations are depending on inventions that have not yet been invented at scale, inventions that are supposed to clear the atmosphere of astronomical amounts of carbon dioxide.

Furthermore, these calculations do not include unforeseen tipping points and feedback loops like the extremely powerful methane gas escaping from rapidly thawing arctic permafrost.

Nor do these scientific calculations include already locked-in warming hidden by toxic air pollution. Nor the aspect of equity – or climate justice – clearly stated throughout the Paris agreement, which is absolutely necessary to make it work on a global scale.

We must also bear in mind that these are just calculations. Estimations. That means that these "points of no return" may occur a bit sooner or later than 2030. No one can know for sure. We can, however, be certain that they will occur approximately in these timeframes because these calculations are not opinions or wild guesses.

These projections are backed up by scientific facts, concluded by all nations through the IPCC. Nearly every single major national scientific body around the world unreservedly supports the work and findings of the IPCC.

Did you hear what I just said? Is my English, OK? Is the microphone on? Because I'm beginning to wonder.

During the last six months, I have travelled around Europe for hundreds of hours in trains, electric cars and buses, repeating these life-changing words over and over again. But no one seems to be talking about it, and nothing has changed. In fact, emissions are still rising. When I have been travelling around to speak in different countries, I am always offered help to write about the specific climate policies in specific countries. But that is not really necessary,

because the basic problem is the same everywhere. And the basic problem is that basically nothing is being done to halt – or even slow – climate and ecological breakdown, despite all the beautiful words and promises.
The UK is, however, very special. Not only for its mind-blowing historical carbon debt but also for its current, very creative, carbon accounting. Since 1990 the UK has achieved a 37% reduction of its territorial CO_2 emissions, according to the Global Carbon Project. And that does sound very impressive. But these numbers do not include emissions from aviation, shipping and those associated with imports and exports. If these numbers are included the reduction is around 10% since 1990 – or an average of 0.4% a year, according to Tyndall Manchester.

And the main reason for this reduction is not a consequence of climate policies, but rather a 2001 EU directive on air quality that essentially forced the UK to close down its very old and extremely dirty coal power plants and replace them with less dirty gas power stations. And switching from one disastrous energy source to a slightly less disastrous one will, of course, result in a lowering of emissions.

But perhaps the most dangerous misconception about the climate crisis is that we have to "lower" our emissions. And that is far from enough. Our emissions have to stop if we are to stay below 1.5-2C of warming. The "lowering of emissions" is, of course, necessary, but it is only the beginning of a fast process that must lead to a stop within a couple of decades *or less. And by "stop" I mean net-zero – and then quickly on to negative figures. That rules out most of today's politics.*

The fact that we are speaking of "lowering" instead of "stopping" emissions is perhaps the greatest force behind the continuing business as usual. The UK's active current support of new exploitation of fossil fuels – for example, the UK shale gas fracking industry, the expansion of its North Sea oil and gas fields, the expansion of airports as well as the planning permission for a brand new coal mine – is beyond absurd. This ongoing irresponsible behaviour will no doubt be remembered in history as one of the greatest failures of humankind. People always tell the other millions of school strikers and me that we should be proud of ourselves for what we have accomplished. But the only thing that we need to look at is the emission curve. And I'm sorry, but it's still rising. That curve is the only thing we should look at.

Every time we make a decision, we should ask ourselves; how will this decision affect that curve? We should no longer measure our wealth and success in the graph that shows economic growth, but in the curve that shows the emissions of greenhouse gases. We should no longer only ask: "Have we got enough money to go through with this?" but also: "Have we got enough of the carbon budget to spare to go through with this?" That should and must become the centre of our new currency.

Many people say that we don't have any solutions to the climate crisis. And they are right. Because, how could we? How do you "solve" the greatest crisis that humanity has ever faced? How do you "solve" a war? How do you "solve" going to the moon for the first time? How do you "solve" inventing new inventions? The climate crisis is both the easiest and the hardest issue we have ever faced. The easiest because we know what we must do. We must stop the emissions of greenhouse gases. The hardest because our current economics are still totally dependent on burning fossil fuels, and thereby destroying ecosystems in order to create everlasting economic growth. "So, exactly how do we solve that?" you ask us – the schoolchildren striking for the climate.

And we say: "No one knows for sure. But we have to stop burning fossil fuels and restore nature and many other things that we may not have quite figured out yet." Then you say: "That's not an answer!" So we say: "We have to start treating the crisis as a crisis – and act even if we don't have all the solutions." "That's still not an answer," you say. Then we start talking about circular economy and rewilding nature and the need for a just transition. Then you don't understand what we are talking about.

We say that all those solutions needed are not known to anyone, and therefore we must unite behind the science and find them together along the way. But you do not listen to that. Because those answers are for solving a crisis that most of you don't even fully understand, or don't want to understand. You don't listen to science because you are only interested in solutions that will enable you to carry on like before, like now. And those answers don't exist anymore. Because you did not act in time, avoiding climate breakdown will require cathedral thinking. We must lay the foundation while we may not know exactly how to build the ceiling.

Sometimes we just simply have to find the way. The moment we decide to fulfil something, we can do anything. And I'm sure that the moment we start behaving as if we were in an emergency, we can avoid climate and ecological catastrophe. Humans are very adaptable: we can still Fix this. But the opportunity to do so will not last for long. We must start today. We have no more excuses. We children are not sacrificing our education, and our childhood for you to tell us what you consider is politically possible in the society that you have created. We have not taken to the streets for you to take selfies with us, and tell us that you really admire what we do. We children are doing this to wake the adults up. We children are doing this for you to put your differences aside and start acting as you would in a crisis. We children are doing this because we want our hopes and dreams back.

I hope my microphone was on. I hope you could all hear me."

LESSONS FROM GRETA

If you carefully read her whole speech transcript, she has multiple times shown the mirror to society and decision-makers in particular, to stand up and *Observe* to be Accountable. Like anything else in the world, people tend to belittle those who stand up and *Observe*. Christopher Caldwell, in his April 2019 write up in The New York Times, says that "her radical approach is at odds with democracy". He goes on to question her maturity as a sixteen-year-old, even to be heard. He calls her "complicated adolescent". He questions her claim to be autistic. He questions her when she calls herself a child since most sixteen years would never do that. He concludes the article by writing "*Democracy often calls for waiting and seeing. Patience may be democracy's cardinal virtue. Climate change is a serious issue. But to say, "We can't wait," is to invite a problem just as grave*". We must always be careful, sensitive and stay clear from those who question us to *Observe* when they decide to look away.

Closer home, two Ambani brothers started a business almost at par post family division. Years later, one who failed to *Observe It*, is struggling not to be declared bankrupt while the other who *Observed It*, created one of the world's largest mobile service company Jio and is the world's 4th wealthiest person.

LESSONS FOR US DURING COVID-19 TIMES

The Covid-19 pandemic has challenged many corporations to re-*Observe* their business models. Travel & Tourism, Hospitality and Aviation are the worst-hit sectors, and the companies in these sectors need to quickly *Observe-It* if they have to continue. Or they face the same fate as Virgin Australia that filed for bankruptcy recently. While this is a severe stressful phase for many industries and the companies, many *Observed-It* quickly and mend their ways. Premium 5-Star rated hotels are offering home delivery of food, large confectionary outlets turned into grocery outlets, and almost everybody started selling sanitisers and masks.

These are examples where businesses *Observe-It* at the right time and mend their ways of doing business for business continuity. Acknowledging *Stuck Clock* behaviour and facing up to "the reality" of the situation takes courage. If we fail to muster that courage, it will result in an unwillingness to pay the price for greater *Accountability* and results. In most difficult situations, we know, in the back of our minds, that acknowledging reality means we'll have to do something about that situation; first, we have to view the situation differently, and then we have to act differently to improve our situation.

RESPONDING TO THE *ACCOUNTABILITY* CRISIS

Viewing a situation differently often means getting comfortable with the fact that we did something wrong, admitting that we could have done more but didn't, or deciding that since we can't do anything to remedy the situation, we may as well move on. Doing something differently about our situation often requires doing things we dislike doing, such as taking a risk we've been avoiding or confronting an issue or person we've been ignoring.

When we permit ourselves to do nothing about our situation when we don't act, don't learn, don't acknowledge our responsibility, don't admit having done wrong, don't face the facts, and don't look for what else we could do to achieve results, our behaviour gets us nowhere. **To get somewhere better, to improve our situation, and to solve our problems, we must abandon the illusion of safety on Stuck Clock and take risks associated with shifting to** *Working Clock.*

When we encounter a difficult situation, we should ask ourselves whether we want to remain in difficulty or attempt some sort of breakthrough to extract ourselves from the situation. To create a better future, we must often break with the past. Failing this, we will, sooner or later, suffer serious consequences for our inaction.

ACCOUNTABILITY QUIZ

Let us take a quiz to see if we are prepared to *Observe* It or we are still stuck in the victim cycle. Give yourself a score of 1 if you agree with the statement, otherwise assign a 0 to it:

1	0	My natural reaction to a setback, is to find someone else for what's happened.
1	0	I won't be able to change my situation myself.
1	0	My thoughts usually begin with phrases like "I can't...", "I'm no good at...", "and I've never been able to ..."
1	0	I often punish myself when things go wrong.
1	0	Mostly I mess up, and bad things happen, but sometimes I'm lucky.
1	0	In the fit of anger, I almost always begin my sentences with "I".
1	0	I usually discuss how hard my life is with my friends.
1	0	I will question and make my friends justify their advice to me as I usually counter it with a "Yes, but..." how do they know my painful situation.
1	0	Analysing past failures and mistakes takes away a fair amount of my time.
1	0	I am always stuck in doing things for a living, there's hardly any time for things I want to do for myself.
1	0	Of course, I need to exercise more and eat healthier, but where's the time right now.
1	0	Owing to my situation of being tied down to all these obligations, I could hardly do some of the things I always think about doing.
1	0	Someday I'll find a new friend who will change my life. In the meantime, hope is my best friend.
1	0	I am only living the negative karma I would have carried form past life.
1	0	I can't be like my friend; I don't have the support he has.

ANALYZING THE RESULT

Total up and see where you are between Zero and Fifteen. Higher the score means, you are still living in the victim of circumstances thinking, that would obstruct your ability to *Observe It*. The big help in accepting the reality of the situation you face can come as feedback from others who know you and your situation well.

The ability to create a better future requires the capacity to acknowledge how you have contributed to your present circumstances. Accepting your mind has contributed to your set of problems, takes power away from the things you may be tempted to blame. This would arm you with the grit to get over your problems.

THE *ACCOUNTABILITY* FEEDBACK

When we accept how we only have contributed to our problems, we work like problem shooters for clues to find out everything that led to our present situation. We should continuously ask for feedback as an investigating officer asks many people to get clues and make a case. A solid case is rarely based on only one or two witnesses. One witness cannot provide a 100% reliable perspective. But the multiple witnesses can provide the common themes leading to compelling evidence of the truth.

Even in personal life, regular feedback with gratitude can work wonders. Requesting and accepting feedback with gratitude is critical to developing personal *Accountability*. One can only improve if one has feedback. Feedback can help you, so treat it like the Gift when you receive it.

Janelle Barlow and Claus Moller, the two authors of the book "*A Complaint is a Gift*" were ahead of their time. They wrote this forward-thinking book around customer feedback way back in 2008 – as the concept of customer feedback as scientific processes was very much in their infancy. Today these concepts are all around us. We're constantly reminded of how important it is to retain customers versus the costs of acquiring new ones.

When giving feedback, we should focus on the behaviour or situation and not the employee. We have to be specific; with an offer of corrective action. Also, make them realise the consequences of continuing with the said behaviour.

You can use this example to understand: "Kabir, as per our company mandate, employees must arrive for work by 9 a.m. In the last week, you arrived at 9:10, 9:15, and 9:05 during the week over three days. You need to make sure to come by or before 9 a.m. If your late coming continues, I'm afraid I'll have to loop HR into our conversation."

While you are seeking feedback for self-development, keep the following points in mind to be effective:

1. **The environment has to be conducive:** a comfortable, quiet place free from interruptions and distractions.

2. **Explain the purpose for whom you are seeking feedback:** Specify how their feedback would help you; it could be of a particular situation or concern.

3. **Listen:** While seeking feedback, actively listen. Even if you strongly disagree with the other person, accept it since you asked for it.

4. **Examples:** Request for specific instances or examples but do not negate it if the other person is unable to provide you.

5. **Gratitude:** Irrespective if the feedback you receive, positive, negative, you agree or disagree, make sure to offer genuine gratitude.

6. **Confidential:** Assure the feedback provider that whatever you discuss remains between two of you, it is only for your self-development, and it should remain that way. Feedback will help you dissect your actions and behaviours to classify for Stuck or *Working Clock*. It will also help you take the facts as is form the horse's mouth.

BENEFITS OF *OBSERVE* PROCESS

CASE STUDY : AUTHOR'S PERSONAL STORY

While we are in the consulting business, we also produce Corporate Videos for our clients. Senior Vice President-Rajiv Shukla of the world's largest luxury car brand is our single point of contact. Rajiv, in turn, reports to Rakesh Sinha, Managing Director of India business. During a couple of internal reviews, we figured out that few of the team members in the client company are not happy with our service, despite us many times going out of our way to support their requirements. After ascertaining all the feedback from the respective consultants of the project, we decided to take action. We decided to practice what we preach to shift to *Working Clock* by first Observing It. We decided to put our point across through an email with a commitment to offering beyond expectation service. We wrote to Rakesh Sinha, with a copy to Rajiv Shukla:

To: Rakesh Sinha
Cc: Rajiv Shukla
Subject: Seventh film production
Dear Mr.Sinha,

We thank you for continuing your trust in us and helping us work on the 7th film in the series of 12 films we are contracted to complete. We appreciate your confidence in our ability to work on various projects with you.

Rajiv has been very helpful, and we can surely say that we cannot work on film projects without his deep technical guidance and vision. However, he is also kind enough to share his constructive feedback with us on his service expectations from us. Rajiv shared that some members of his team have not been able to reach us for a few requirements. Some of them feel that we are not as accessible, as they would like us to be.

This is a deeply concerning area for us as we take pride in our service response time. We assure you that we will do everything to remove such an impression and live up to our name. Your feedback is a wake-up call for us, and it will not only help us improve but also grow. Towards that, we have taken the following steps:

We will set up a weekly project review with Rajiv and his team to not only review the progress but also to address any concerns in our deliverables on time. Owing to our Coaching practice, Sandeep and I may not be able to take the calls when in a session. However, anyone from Rajiv's team can call our office number and leave a message to call back, and we will revert by the end of the day.

We are also deputing Nidhi from our office, who would be in touch with Rajiv regularly to address any requirement or update us.

At any point in time, you face trouble in accessibility, tell us so at once through SMS/WhatsApp, and we will revert latest by the end of the day.

We need your valuable feedback to foster our Accountability for results. We look forward to our ongoing relationship and continue to meet your objectives.

Warm Regards

ROLE OF INTENT AND ACTION

While some may argue about what's great in this, it is just a normal communication, but it did communicate our intent to remove the client's perception. It conveys our concern on their feedback and also our resolve with specific steps towards the solution. It communicates that we can *Observe* and are committed to *Own* before *Fixing* and making it a *Repeat* practice. A couple of months later, we received a new film project from this firm.

We had the choice to just overlook and continue as normal. That approach might have cost us our biggest client. This approach helped us move towards *Working Clock* that left positive feedback with our client and also helped us enhance our relationship with more business.

CIRCLING BACK TO MAHABHARATA

Before we move on to the next chapter to understand the next step for shifting to *Working Clock*, lets us see what did various characters do or not do to *Own* up. What sets the ground for the epic Mahabharata, because the main players refused to *Own* up.

Bhishma, Drona, and other elders did not refuse to *Own* up; they did *Own* up, but they did not *Own* up to *Fix*. Draupadi, who was the queen of emperor Yudhishthira, was a honourable person. To dishonour such a person and dragging in the assembly by the hair remains the most horrendous act. Pandavas can lose everything in the gambling match, including themselves, but they do not have the authority to gamble their wives, which they did. Kaurava's including Duryodhan, Dushasana, Karna, and Shakuni who were blinded to disrepute Pandavas in whatever possible way lead to the most heinous act of disrobing Draupadi.

Draupadi tried her best by holding on to a technicality and questioned if Yudhishthira has gambled himself first and lost then how he could have gambled me afterwards. Draupadi tried her best to get out of the situation; she could clearly see she was in. Dhritarashtra, who was the King of Hastinapur and the father of the Kauravas, was the most powerful person in the hall. As a king, he was meant to oppose this disgraceful act and *Own* up the consequences; instead, he decided to look the other way owing to his greed for the throne and the desire to displace the Pandavas.

One of the elders, Vidura, not only *Observed* but also tried to *Own* up the consequence. He vehemently protested this act, but since he did not have any influential political position owing to his being a stepbrother from a servant, his dissent was not considered. Vidura tried his best to explain, quoting scriptures. That any innocent victim when approaches this assembly is assured of justice. The denial of justice can curse the assembly, and those entrusted to give justice will bear serious consequences. However, Dhritarashtra remained adamantly 'blind' and 'deaf'.

Bhishma, at his level, tried his best to reason out with Draupadi. He told her that the question raised by her are very difficult to answer. One side Yudhishthira upheld his self-esteem by losing everything in the gamble but his wife. It's only the devious plan of revenge of Shakuni that prompted Yudhishthira to take a chance to gain back everything that he had lost. It is wrong on Draupadi's part to think that she is a 'property' of Yudhishthira; instead, an Indian wife is always considered equal to her husband. This argument clearly demonstrates how Bhishma failed to *Observe* and *Own* the future consequences that were clearly visible to Vidura.

One of the Kaurava brothers, Vikarna, tried to *Observe* and *Own*, who was against the evil disposition of the Kauravas. He not only objected but also said that the whole match was null and void because Yudhishthira was compelled to gamble. He argued that the gamble was between Duryodhan and Yudhishthira, but Shakuni played the dice for Duryodhan, and that's against the rule. He also repeated Draupadi's technical point that how someone can lose her when he had already lost everything that belonged to him; hence the whole match should be declared null and void.

Externally, Bhishma was focussed on the letter of the law while forgetting the spirit. The wife belongs to the husband means that the wife is under the protection of the husband. Protection is required by weak people, in this situation, Draupadi. However, owing to Bhishma and Dronacharya's allegiance to the King, they went with the letter of the law instead of the spirit. Thus they not only refused to *Observe* the inevitable but also refused to *Own* up the future. How would they be remembered centuries later?

CHAPTER

5

Own

Krishna protected Draupadi, her sister, and saved her honour. He ignored the technicality about who behaved in what way and why they behaved like that. Therefore, the surrender of Draupadi to Krishna and Krishna's reciprocation is the purpose of this story. This epic helps us to understand the deeper nuances of *Own* it up in the real world.

CURRENT REALITY

Too many Indians have lost the heart to own their circumstances, and that nature has begun eroding the very foundation of society. Covid-19 has multiplied the problems to the next level. Stable jobs are disappearing; the working class is starting to adjust to a fragile and frightening New Normal. This New Normal is the new metaphysics of work. Companies are portable, and workers are throwaway. People are talking about the GIG economy where nothing is permanent. All services are available on-demand. Companies are waking up to the reality that perhaps half of the employees need not attend office. Second thought, why do we need employees? The rise of the knowledge economy means a change, in less than 20 years, from an overbuilt system of large, slow-moving economic units to an array of small, widely dispersed financial centres, some as small as the solopreneur. In the gig economy, geography dissolves, the highways are bandwidth. People are questioning the existence of all physical things.

WAY FORWARD

Companies across India and the rest of the world, have already informed their staff to work from home till the end of the year. Work from home trend began around March 2020. We are experiencing this trend while writing this book in the second half of the year 2020.

Large IT multinationals like Google, Microsoft, and many others have 'allowed' work from home till March 2021.

Companies are exploring all options to survive and then grow. India's largest staffing firm, Team Lease Limited initiated this trend of providing temp workers. As we advance, this trend is only going to expand. In fact, for a lot of projects, companies are seeking gig workers on the world's largest professional platform, LinkedIn.

World's largest taxi service company does not own a single car (Uber). World's largest market place doesn't have any store (Amazon). World's largest travel & stay company does not own any property (Airbnb). The world's most extensive set of data and information is on 'cloud' (Google).

America's iconic Detroit city that was known as the mecca for automobiles is getting replaced with Tesla. The astonishing fact is that an electric car has only 10% of the automative parts compared to a conventional vehicle. Temporary or gig worker's ranks are multiplying, and one can expect them to outnumber permanent full-time workers by 2025.

Employees are going to have to create their own lives, their careers, and their successes. Some people may go kicking and screaming into the new world. There is only one clear message there: You're now in business for yourself. In this scenario, *Owning* up for every worker would become more critical compared to 'safe' jobs.

One of the first requirements after *Owning* it, is to apologize, irrespective of your position. Here's an example of *Owning* It Up.

CASE STUDY : AIRBNB STORY

In Dec 2015, Airbnb, the home-sharing platform, got into controversy for racial profiling and discrimination taking place on their site. The same month, researchers from Harvard released a working paper indicating that travellers with *"distinctively African-American names are 16% less likely to be accepted relative to identical guests with distinctively White names."* That research was sufficient to compound and ignited the social media to share stories from travellers who experienced that discrimination first-hand, as well as a lawsuit over such actions.

Going by the social media dialogue, it appears that the issue is not yet entirely resolved. However, Airbnb never tried to dodge and was quite proactively in addressing the big problem. Airbnb's Co-founder and CEO, Brian Chesky, began with this email:

Dear Airbnb community,

At the heart of our mission is the idea that people are fundamentally good and every community is a place where you can belong. We don't say this because it sounds nice. It's the goal that everyone at Airbnb works towards every day – because we've all seen how when we live together, we better understand each other.

Discrimination is the opposite of belonging, and its existence on our platform jeopardizes this core mission. Bias and discrimination have no place on Airbnb, and we have zero tolerance for them. Unfortunately, we have been slow to address these problems, and for this I am sorry. I take responsibility for any pain or frustration this has caused members of our community. We will not only make this right; we will work to set an example that other companies can follow.

In June, we asked Laura Murphy, the former head of the American Civil Liberties Union's Washington D.C. Legislative Office, to review every aspect of the Airbnb platform, and to make sure that we're doing everything we can to fight bias and discrimination. Thanks to Laura's leadership, today we're releasing a report that outlines the results of that process. You can read the full report here, but I'd like to highlight four changes that will impact the way our platform works:

Airbnb Community Commitment

Beginning November 1, everyone who uses Airbnb must agree to a stronger, more detailed nondiscrimination policy. We aren't just

Chesky begins the letter and acknowledges the mistake of Airbnb. He acknowledged that the brand was far too slow to respond to the issue of discrimination, and apologized for it. Post that, the company has taken several actions to prevent and put an end to it on the platform. A 32-page report written by Laura W. Murphy, director of the ACLU's Washington Legislative Office also support these action. The report referred an audit to assess where Airbnb was falling short on thwarting discrimination, and the subsequent measures that would be in place. After the report went public, the company launched a publicity campaign on a platform of inclusion. They also ran an advertisement that aired during the 2017 Super Bowl (Super Bowl is the annual championship game of the National Football League played in early February. It is the culmination of a regular season that begins in the late summer of the previous year).

Airbnb provided an inspiring example of what's the first requirement to *Own* what you *Observe*.

SELECTIVE *ACCOUNTABILITY*

If one selectively assume *Accountability* for some of their circumstances and conveniently reject it for others, one cannot stay on the steps to *Accountability*. Selective perception prevents people from owning their contribution to the creation of their circumstances and also keeps them mired in the victim cycle, as the following disguised but true story aptly illustrates.

CASE STUDY : SUNIL DIXIT STORY

After completing his professional qualifications in cost and works management Sunil Dixit accepted a good job offer of an accountant in a mid-size manufacturing company. He worked there for about five years before meeting Suraj from his institute. Suraj was working in one of the large media company's print division in the sales department. Suraj knew that Sunil is a performer and is known for getting into key details to be successful. Suraj also kept Sunil's qualifications and experience in mind. He invited Sunil for a short meeting to discuss a key position in his company.

THEY MET AND DISCUSSED AS [TRANSCRIPT BELOW]:

Suraj: Thanks for coming over, such a pleasure to meet after so many years. I still have those fond memories of having tea at the neighbourhood tea stall during breaks. So, how's your job going on?

Sunil: Yeah, what days we had, not only tea but also those frequent picnics in the group. I guess that's life, and those memories would always remain with us to cherish for a lifetime. My job is fine with routine affairs, almost mechanical life. But it's a good company, and they have given me my dues in recognition as well as money. You tell me, how are things at your end professionally?

Suraj: Oh, great! I am very happy as sales give in a different kick on every closure. The brand name is such that we don't have to work hard to convince the buyers. The company has great performance-linked incentives. I can save almost my entire salary as I manage my expenses through the incentives I earn. We are coming up with a new offering for people. This would be the first time that we will be tying up with our closest competitor to block another big media house that is aspiring to enter the newspaper business. This has opened up a lot of opportunities for good people. I would suggest you think about it and come over. The media is going to be very big in the coming days. Ours is a diversified group into newspapers, radio, digital, events, education, and many more divisions. This gives us the benefit of exploring options within the group.

Sunil: This is great; I am so happy to know that you are not only growing but also enjoying and earning well. You would know that manufacturing may not give such a variety of options. Plus I have a stable job here, and I have aligned my lifestyle with whatever I earn.

Suraj: Sure, I understand that manufacturing has its stability. However, as you said, I think it does becomes mechanical after a while. I know we both have studied the same, and a lot of people look for a stable job after that qualification. However, I think I took a wise decision to join Sales, and I am so happy on all counts. I think you have it in you to explore; I mean what stops you from not having a happening life me.

Sunil: Perhaps you are right, my wife is in Sales, and she always reminds me that I should have followed you. But you know how these decisions pan out. However, after talking to you, now I have two very close people who are pushing me to Sales. So, if anything goes wrong, you two will be responsible, ha-ha.

Suraj: I have confidence in you that you would do a great job. By the way, I need to know what salary you draw as I need to discuss with my VP and he would ask me. Also, what's the title you hold?

Sunil: I am at Rupees Thirty lakh per annum, all-inclusive, and a Deputy General Manager

Suraj: Oh, I am at Rupees Forty Lakh salary and get additional incentives. Next year I would be Associate Vice President with a minimum Rupees Sixty Lakh per year package. That's why I am telling you to think about it. After all, this is our age to work hard and grow fast.

Sunil: Yes, I agree that this is our age to grow and take risks.

Suraj: Great, then let me talk to my Vice President and *Fix* the interview.

Sunil came back home thinking about the lifestyle, confidence, and the money Suraj was making. Just five years ago, they started their career together. He suddenly started looking at a brighter future. He went home and told his wife, and she was thrilled. At the same time, she thanked Suraj that what she could not achieve; Suraj has done it. Three days later, he received a call from Suraj's office. Vice President's secretary called and told Sunil to come for an interview next week to Mumbai. She also mentioned that after he confirms, she will arrange his flight tickets and the Vice President would meet him at the airport only as he would be at the airport around at the time of Sunil's flight arrival.

Sunil could not believe how things moved so fast. He thought perhaps this is what had to happen and he was unnecessary skeptical about Suraj. He called Suraj and informed him everything with a confirmation that he would be coming to Mumbai for meeting the VP. Sural told him that he is so happy to know that and would love to see him, but he would be in Singapore for a launch event during that time. Suraj assured Sunil that he is confident that everything would go positive and he should now start looking at better days ahead.

Sunil arrived at the Mumbai airport through morning flight to meet the VP. He was pleasantly surprised to see that the VP was there to receive him with his driver holding the placard. VP, Rane appeared as warm-hearted as he welcomed Sunil with a great handshake and a big smile. Sunil was impressed to see his BMW-7 car.

So, Rane started as soon as they sat at the back seat of the luxury car. "Sunil, Suraj told me about you, and I am excited to meet you. I have a meeting in next hour at the Hyatt where you would be staying overnight to fly back tomorrow. So, I thought let's use this time to meet up". Sunil has stayed in good hotels but staying in a luxury hotel like Hyatt in Mumbai, was something he never thought about. Rane continued "so, let's come straight to the point. We are very happy to have Suraj in our team, and he is doing so well. He has given us strong positive feedback about you, and we are always looking out for good people. However, I understand that you have never worked in Sales. But that's not an issue as Suraj when he joined had no Sales experience. Look at him today, and he is a rock star of my team. Sunil, I want you to take charge of Sales for our new offering we are coming up next month. You will have the choice to bring your family here and stay in a three-bedroom flat at Worli, or you can go back to your family every weekend with all expenses paid. You decide what works best for you. However, we need someone to get on the job quickly and take away the burden from my shoulders as I need to focus on the Singapore event where Suraj is today. So, you take a rest and perhaps we meet again in the evening for dinner as I would be closing my meeting by seven". Sunil could not comprehend what all was happening around him. It appeared too good to be happening. He compared with his own company where people have to get approvals to even book an air-conditioned train journey. Even his top management never stays in luxury hotels. Sunil was almost in a dream situation. After some time Rane and Sunil got down at the hotel, and Rane took leave from him while directing him to reception to check-in.

Sunil went to his room that was a suite. The first thing he did is made a video call to his wife and showed the opulence of the luxury suite. His wife could not believe that he was staying there and told him that she would like to stay whenever they visit Mumbai next. Sunil was elated, and he didn't know how to react. He thought this could be a life-changing opportunity for him. Around four he received a call from Rane's secretary that he would be waiting for him to have dinner together at the Cellini, signature Italian restaurant at Hyatt and he should keep himself ready. Sunil was not fond of Italian food, but he had no choice.

Sunil went to the restaurant five minutes before and welcomed Rane as he came in at sharp 7 pm. Sunil asked him "May I know few more details about the offer", "sure, I'll be happy to answer", replied Rane. Sunil asked him "Why do you think that I would be a good Salesperson, while I have never been in Sales?" Rane laughed and said "Suraj told me about your capabilities and Sales my friend is not rocket science. We need people who can think logically and eventually become business heads. Rest assured the concerns you have would soon evaporate as you start tasting success. Let's order for dinner first. I am a vegetarian, you can have non-vegetarian as I don't mind." Sunil also opted for vegetarian and Rane ordered 3-4 dishes that Sunil had no idea. Sunil again started "so, what about the compensation?" Rane said "I am sorry, I thought somebody from HR would have spoken and explained. Anyways, you will start with rupees thirty-five lakh as *Fixed* salary plus you will have the opportunity to earn an additional fifteen lakh since it's a new launch and we have kept handsome incentives. What do you say about that offer?" Sunil, could not believe that he could be earning almost similar to Suraj. He immediately responded, "thank you I think that's a good enough offer for me." Rane said "great than let's get started, you join as soon as possible, maybe within a week". Sunil said, he has to serve a one month notice to which Rane said that's not an issue as they would buy that out. So, practically he can join from next day. Sunil could not believe that everything was happening so fast. While the one side he was thinking is it worth taking such a big risk of shifting from his stable job and another side he was lured by the lifestyle and money. He decided to go with the offer as he might have to wait for at least three more years to get that kind of package. He called his wife and informed her that he had accepted the offer from the company and he would visit her every weekend for a year till he settles and later she can quit and join him in Mumbai.

January 1, Sunil joined the company, and he was so happy to work in a dynamic environment with all support coming his way. Rane was also very helpful whenever Sunil required him. With his people beating their sales targets, he knew he had made the right career choice. He and his wife started to plan when his wife can quit her job and move to Mumbai. They decided that she need not work since Sunil was earning enough to have a good life and also have savings.

April 1 Sunil was shattered hearing about the rumour that the division he was managing has been sold to a competitor. Instead of relying upon rumours, he called Rane to enquire. Rane said "yes you heard it right, it's part of business strategy. We have negotiated a kind of barter with the competition where they exit one of our competing businesses, and we exit this one." Rane assured him that the company which is taking over is equally good and he should not have any issues." Sunil felt betrayed and called his wife to inform. His wife's first reaction was that thankfully she had not left the job. Sunil told her that it's not that his job is lost, but the future is uncertain.

Next few months Sunil saw key people of his team leave, and he was managing the not so great people from the company that took over. His new supervisor was nowhere in the league of Rane. He always used to remind Sunil that he is one of the highest-paid employees. Sunil tried his best to motivate the new team, but he realized owing to culture, they just don't understand the importance of going all out for it. Sunil regretted why he ventured at all in the new line. During the first half-yearly review, his new supervisor Bhalerao told him that Sunil's performance is not up to the mark and they have to restructure his package to reduce the *Fix*ed component. Sunil challenged Bhalerao with all reasons why the situation is bad, but Bhalerao was in no mood to hear anything and told Sunil that he should get the new letter from HR by evening. After receiving the letter Sunil was shocked, his weekly Delhi trip was removed as a perk, he was now supposed to pay 50% of the rent of the flat he stays in Worli. His incentives would now only qualify on 100% achievement instead of starting from 50% target achievement. When he computed the entire redesigned offer, he realized that it was at the same level as his last job.

Almost finding himself lost, he thought of Suraj. He called to check if they can meet and Suraj agreed wholeheartedly. When they met at a restaurant on Juhu beach, Sunil almost pinned the blame on Suraj that he is in this situation because of him. Suraj was a little surprised, but he remained calm and asked Sunil "tell me what's your contribution to the new company that took over your division? I know a lot of people there, and they told me that you were trying to use the same techniques of this company there. How do you expect results knowing that the culture of that company is different? Like you enjoyed the culture at my company after leaving the older company. You successfully made the transition. Why could you not do that with the new company? And you are narrating the story to me as if you could not have done anything." Suraj and Sunil kept discussing it over the week, and Suraj made Sunil realize that somewhere Sunil failed to Observe and Own up the situation.

When Suraj told Sunil that he should rewind and look for situations that may have led to this, Sunil realized the warning signs he missed. Rane had informed sometime back that they might offload this business owing to bottom-line pressure. Sunil ignored the first warning sign. When two months ago he had an issue with the bathroom heater of his apartment, he ignored the receipt that mentioned it as a monthly renewal contract and not a standard eleven months rent agreement. He also overlooked a speeding challan of his company car that was from a leasing company and not a company-Owned car as he had in his last company. Sunil also failed to adapt to the new culture as smoothly as he did when he joined this company. He always had some kind of apprehension about the new employer and hence never gave his 100%.

So, is Sunil, therefore accountable for what eventually happened to him? Yes, in so many ways. While he enjoyed the benefits of a new job, great supervisor, great entitlements, he failed to transfer the same zeal with the new employer. Sunil learned through objective self-assessment that he must shoulder some responsibility. After Sunil spoke to Suraj and pondered Suraj's feedback, he finally came to appreciate both points of view: that of the victim and that of the accountable individual. Eventually, Sunil was ready to own his circumstances and create a better future. However, not many people take this step toward greater *Accountability*.

CASE STUDY : LESSONS FROM JACK MA

Amongst all the examples of succeeding by failing, perhaps Jack Ma is the best example. Twice he failed in primary school. Thrice he failed in middle school. He had to appear thrice for his university entrance exam. Police force rejected him for hiring, and so did KFC. In KFC out of the 24 applicants, 23 were selected, and he was the only one rejected. His best failure was perhaps Harvard, where he applied ten times and was continuously rejected every time.

Today, Jack Ma is one of the richest and most successful people in the world. He founded Alibaba, which is one of the largest e-commerce companies on the planet. Jack Ma, twice made it to the Time magazine's "100 most influential people", in 2009 and 2014. He was also selected as one of 'China's Most Powerful People' by Businessweek. He also appeared on the front page of Forbes magazine.

HUMBLE BEGINNINGS

At the time of the Cultural Revolution, Jack Ma was born in the city of Hangzhou in China and grew up in a poor family. During the visit of US President Richard Nixon to Hangzhou in 1972, Jack Ma became spellbound by the Western world. As a young child, he started visiting hotels where US tourists stayed. He requested to learn English from them in exchange for giving them tours around the city. While being friends with one of the tourists, Jack Ma got his English name 'Jack'.

Jack did not give up after failing his university entrance exam twice, scoring less than 1% in math. As he was committed to studying English, he eventually passed. After that, he began studying English at the Hangzhou Teacher's Institute. His troubles did not stop there, as after graduating, he applied for 30 different types of jobs but could not get even one. He was eventually able to find a job as an English teacher, that made him earn as little as US$ 12 per month.

DETERMINATION THROUGH FAILURE

All the failures and rejections did not break Jack's determination, and he persisted throughout. Equipped with his English skills in China, Jack Ma launched a translation service business that took him to the US as a translator. In that trip, he was introduced to the internet. Jack did not have any technical knowledge of computers or coding, but that did not stop his interest in the new phenomenon called internet, at the time.

While trying to find Chinese beer in online search and failing, he thought of creating an online store for it. The success made him create his second initiative online called 'Chinapage' that listed Chinese businesses and products. This small idea led to a flood of emails from all over the world from people seeking to get into partnerships. To continue expanding and growing, he took the help of a government company for funding. Over a period of time, the partner company gained majority control over the business and led to his eventual departure from the company.

Having lost in business, Jack Ma decided to take up a government job at the Ministry for Foreign Trade and Economic Cooperation. This job provided an opportunity for Jack to build connections with people of influence. One such influencer turned out to be the founder of Yahoo!, Jerry Yang. Jack Ma proposed to set up an online marketplace after his search for Chinese beer did not show anything in the search results'

THE ASCEND TO SUCCESS

In 1999, after having left the government job, Ma gathered a group of seventeen of his friends and pitched the idea of an online marketplace for small and medium-sized businesses. To secure funding for this venture, Ma travelled to the US once again, this time to Silicon Valley to pitch his idea. But he faced a familiar obstacle as his idea was rejected and criticized as being unprofitable and unsustainable. Through persistence, Ma was eventually able to secure funding of US$ 5 million from Goldman Sachs and US$ 20 million from Softbank.

However, in 2003, the future still looked bleak for Alibaba, with the company failing to make any revenue within the first three years and facing bankruptcy within eighteen months. As the Chinese economy was still in its infancy at the time, businesses and government authorities were sceptical about the idea of an online marketplace. Ma also faced internal issues within Alibaba, as part of his vision for the company to grow and attract young, outside talent required limiting his existing venture partners' promotions to ranks above managerial roles. Unintentionally, this resulted in dissension amongst a number of his team who ended up walking out on him.

MAKING HISTORY

But Ma was able to pick up the pieces and unify his remaining team to take Alibaba forward, challenging established online businesses like eBay who already had existing operations in China. Within five years, Ma and Alibaba managed to drive eBay out of business in China, and with the help of further funding from Yahoo! founder Jerry Yang, Alibaba was able to expand and grow further into the international market. In 2014, Alibaba made history through the world's largest IPO to date. The company has continued to grow from strength to strength, scaling its operations into various industries such as technology and logistics, turning the online business into one of the world's largest conglomerates today.

BOTH SIDES OF THE STORY

Unlike, Jack Ma, millions of people keep themselves from achieving the results and happiness they so desperately pursue because of their unwillingness to see both sides of the story and "own" their circumstances. Perhaps they give up so soon.

Like Yudhishthira in Mahabharata, too often, such people blame their lack of happiness on perplexing circumstances that seem totally beyond their control. Rather than own their circumstances by seeing the whole story, they choose to view themselves as incapable of modifying their situations through their actions, resigning themselves to being "acted upon" by influences and forces rather than the other way around. Ultimately, who stopped him from taking charge and refuse to play the *Dyut Krida* (gambling) with Duryodhan supported by Shakuni.

In a different example, Delhi Metro Rail Corporation (DMRC) chief E. Sreedharan, though not directly responsible, owned the "moral responsibility" and stepped down after the worst accident in the history of Delhi Metro. Six people were killed and 15 injured when an elevated section of the tracks under construction came crashing down in July of 2009. DMRC Chief later took back his resignation. Unfortunately, the same site had another accident when cranes involved in the operation crashed at the site the next day of the accident. The second incident left six workers injured. Senior official Vijay Anand, director (projects) with the DMRC, told news reporters that as second-in-charge of the project (Central Secretariat to Badarpur stretch) he had owned "moral responsibility" and asked to be sent back to the Indian Railways. He was appointed director (projects) in October 2007. The Central Secretariat-Badarpur line was under Anand's supervision — he was responsible for the planning and design execution of the corridor. DMRC sources said Anand was responsible for overlooking the clean-up operations after the first accident.

As per RTI (Right To Information), in 16 years of Metro construction in Delhi, as many as 156 people working at DMRC died due to mishaps during construction. The data also reveals that 103 workers were injured in the construction work in the same period. "To increase efficiency and accuracy, DMRC many times ignored rules under the Labour Law, increasing pressure on the employees. Most employees are overburdened," said a member of the DMRC Staff Council, which was constituted to take care of employees' complaints and grievances. "We at DMRC follow international norms of safety during construction. Any death is unfortunate, but fatalities do take place. Each case is investigated. It is needless to say that we take care of our staff," said Anuj Dayal Chief, public relations officer, DMRC. This type is the difference of Owning up by the people at senior leadership positions and those in public relations.

The situation in the private, corporate sector is not entirely different. Even in most professional companies, it is seldom that post any accident any particular department would rise to take ownership. The first reaction is to "find out" whodunit. Many times when people decide to look another way to *Own* up, the competition gets very aggressive. It starts to impact the company that awaits the "result of the findings". By that time competition dents their share of the market and makes consumers accept the new product easily.

Not all brands face that threat, though. One of the oldest beverage brands in India (and Pakistan) is an iconic brand from the house of Hamdard. Rooh Afza, which in Urdu means 'something that refreshes the soul' . It was created in 1908 by Hakim Hafiz Abdul Majeed, as a herbal option to beat the heat. Rooh Afza was created using herbs and syrups from traditional Unani medicine. It was originally introduced as a medicine to counter heat strokes, reduce palpitation, and prevent water loss. Popular household drink Rooh Afza had gone missing from Indian store shelves in the summer of 2019, at a time when soaring temperatures spruce up demand for the rose-flavoured beverage. While reports blamed the supply shortages on a family rift, the company had dismissed the theory. Hamdard Laboratories (India), the manufacturer of Rooh Afza, had stopped production of the drink in November 2018 citing the shortage of crucial herbal ingredients.

The shortage affected many people, with many taking to Twitter to rue its absence during the Muslim fasting month of Ramzan, in which Rooh Afza is considered a staple fare at the Iftaar (when the day-long Ramzan fast is broken). The Indian market was flooded by Rooh Afza manufactured by Hamdard Pakistan and brought in by importers, a bottle of which costs a steep Rs 350, compared to Rs 135 for the Indian version. Hamdard Pakistan, which does not officially export to India, had offered to export the required quantities for the Ramzan period.

We are citing this recent Rooh Afza example to explain how the market is always looking at pouncing on the established brands. A small gap, irrespective of the reasons are always up for attack from the competition. Markets are unapologetic and ruthless; they do not wait long to replace. Therefore, any issue at the company must be communicated with customers with the steps being taken and when can customers expect the product back.

ACCOUNTABILITY PITSTOP

Before moving ahead, you may like to assess how strongly you perceive the following ten areas. Try to list down highlighting the blockages you face on the following:

TEN FACTS ABOUT MYSELF:

1. I know about the Vision of the organisation

2. I am Involved in Goal Setting and Planning Activities

3. Explain Why (for #2, don't just take decisions but explain)

4. I can choose How

5. I delegate Authority (not only tasks)

6. I Trust, before I have to

7. I Encourage people to solve their problems, themselves

8. I hold people Accountable

9. I provide Constructive Feedback

10. I acknowledge on the spot

Once you are done filling the above, move to the next step in finding if you are in the victim or circumstances driven behaviours. Or you are on *Working Clock* and taking steps to be accountable.

For each of the above ten statements, keep the following in mind

- Did you pretend that there were things you pretended, not to know?
- Did you seek clarity for above
- Did you take some extra steps to help you get a better outcome?
- Could there be some facts you are ignoring (or ignored)?
- Do you think you could have spoken to some people that you

might have avoided too?

- How often you feel the same?
- Is there learning to apply?
- Could you see that perhaps some of your behaviours or actions were preventing you from getting the desired results?

Now, score yourself between 1-10 keeping the above points in mind. Needless to say, be honest with yourself:

1. I am clear about the Vision of the organization - Score [   ]
2. I am Involved in Goal Setting and Planning Activities - Score [   ]
3. Explain Why (for #2, don't just take decisions but explain) - Score [   ]
4. I can choose How Score - [   ]
5. I delegate Authority (not only tasks) - Score [   ]
6. I Trust, before I have to - Score [   ]
7. I Encourage people to solve their problems, themselves - Score [   ]
8. I hold people Accountable - Score [   ]
9. I provide Constructive Feedback - Score [   ]
10. I acknowledge on the spot - Score [   ]

Add up all the scores you gave yourself between 1-10 statements. Follow the below scale to see how Accountable you are:

80-100 You see yourself quite Accountable by Owning your circumstances

50-70 Means you on the average scale, meaning you oscillate between Owning or avoiding

10-40 Indicates that you are still on *Stuck Clock*. You feel that it's not you but circumstances that stop you in taking Ownership.

A low score indicates that you are failing to stand up and assume Ownership for the situation. However, it may also indicate that you are truly in a situation that's beyond your control. Even if that's the case, a person who *Owns* the circumstances either works to change them or finds another place to come out of the stuck zone. Imagine yourself, someone, continuously cribbing about any issue being faced, even after you provided some options towards resolution. There would be a time, you would start avoiding the person.

HOW OWNERSHIP HELPS BIOLOGICALLY

Dopamine, oxytocin, serotonin, and endorphins (every so often referred to as D.O.S.E.) are four predominant chemicals that can drive the positive emotions you feel throughout the day. Out of these four chemicals, serotonin is a social chemical, but it functions in an altogether distinct way. Pride, loyalty and status get impacted with the serotonin. Effects of Serotonin is felt when we feel a sense of accomplishment or recognition from others. This could be from receiving your diploma, crossing the finish line in a race, or being appreciated for hard work in the office. Serotonin can create strong, positive emotions.

Interestingly, serotonin can help build both sides of social dynamics. Serotonin is what motivates a leader to excel and grow their influence - to win awards and become popular in the news. But serotonin also compels their followers to do well - to not let down their leader, parent, or teacher and excel in life. This last property helps magically. Ownership is so closely related to this chemical. When we get a dose of this chemical by Ownership, it also impacts others around. It works like a SMILE; rarely one would get a frown response to a smile. Let us see this example on how it can affect a whole society:

FIFA World Cup 2018 set a great example where football fans from Japan had stayed back after the matches. They were there to clean up the garbage inside the stadiums. Japanese fans continued the ritual despite their national team bowing out of the world cup after a facing a 3-2 loss from Belgium in the round of 16 at Rostov-On-Don city. Japan was the only Asian team carrying the hopes of millions of people in the round of 16. Unfortunately, their dream run was stopped by Belgium. Belgium in the process became the first team to recover from a situation of two goals down to win a World Cup knockout round match after Germany's 3-2 win over England in the 1970 World Cup. Even after getting knocked out from last-16 match, the Japanese team fans started cleaning themselves. They started picking up litter in their section of the Rostov Arena Stadium from under the seats. The Japanese team was underdogs with their 61st-ranking, and they had very little chance of leaving an impact at the world cup tournament. Their valiant group stage matches and last-16 meet versus Belgium won hearts.

While the players won laurels for their performance on the field, the Japanese fans left with respect and praise from all over the world with their kind gesture off the field and have now set a great example for the fans of other teams that are remaining in the tournament. Cleanliness is something that the Japanese are very particular about even back home as it is ingrained in their culture. "Cleaning the school is a part of the school day and an aspect of the education that students receive," explains Scott North, who is a professor of sociology at Osaka University. "Cleaning up contributes to keeping the environment livable in the densely populated cities and is also an expression of care and regard for one's neighbours. I think the Japanese are proudly conscious of their reputation as a clean culture, and they probably expect other places to be somewhat less so," he added further. This also gets linked to the Ownership of their actions and culture. It impacted many non-Japanese to follow them in cleaning their litter.

The fruits of owning your circumstances more than compensate for the heart-rending effort involved. You change the circumstances for better when you find the heart to own your circumstances; you automatically gain the commitment to overcome and change those circumstances. And this serotonin chemical starts to spread.

THE NEXT STEP TOWARDS *ACCOUNTABILITY*

Lord Krishna in Mahabharata had to spend about 45 minutes to make Arjun not only realize that he carries the Ownership to end the wrong but also *Fix* the situation he is in. In the forthcoming chapter, we will understand how *Observe* and *Own* behaviours help one to *Fix* for removing the obstacles on the path of success.

CHAPTER

6

Fix

Yatra yogeshvara kiho yatra pārtho dhanur-dhara
tatra śhrīr vijayo bhūtir dhruvā nītir matir mama

Where Krishna, the Lord of Yogins remains,
where the son of Parth holds his bow, there lie fortune,
victory, prosperity, and firm justice-so I believe.

One of the last shlokas in Gita emphasises the importance of *Fixing* what Arjun has *Observed* and takes the *Ownership* to correct. The shloka is considered to be one of the most powerful shlokas in Gita, and a lot of people advise to recite it daily to be mindful and successful. There comes a time in the Mahabharata epic when Arjun seeing all his relatives, elders and cousins are his opponents is stressed and he asks Krishna, why should he kill his own? To which Krishna reminds Arjun of his duty to *Fix* the injustice.

Krishna invokes the concept of *Dharma*, sacred duty, which sustains the cosmic order. This *Dharma* differs according to the class and caste into which a person is born. As a member of the warrior class, Arjun has the primary sacred duty of fighting righteous battles. Therefore he must, by all means, fight. Look to your duty; do not tremble before it; nothing is better for a warrior than a battle of sacred duty. If you fail to *Fix* this war of sacred duty, you will abandon your duty and fame, only to gain evil. Your duty done imperfectly is better than another man's done well. It is better to die in one's duty; another man's duty is perilous.

This key message in Gita makes us understand the importance of *Fixing* it, ourselves instead of waiting or hoping from others. Japanese, did not forget to *Fix* it, even after losing the qualification game in the football world cup.

The 35 million cases of COVID-19 and about a million fatalities due to SARS-CoV-2 (numbers as of this writing) could have been greatly controlled. The viral upsurge could have been stopped in December 2019 in Wuhan if we had the circumspection and financial approvals to develop antiviral drugs or vaccines.

In the aftermath of the SARS-CoV pandemic of 2003, wildlife sampling taught us that bats harbour many SARS-like coronaviruses. Successive research divulged that some of these bat viruses have global epidemic potential. We knew that CoVs loitered in bats in China with the capacity to cause an epidemic. However, no one would invest the money needed to make antiviral drugs or vaccines.

After SARS-CoV, big pharma lost interest in the virus – because it had disappeared from the face of the Earth. However, several laboratories around the world continued their research on the virus. Big pharma could see that there was no money to be made in SARS-CoV antivirals or vaccines; hence none were made. Only when SARS-CoV-2 emerged in late 2019 with inexorable spread around the globe, humanity realised that it just could not stop it. We failed to *Fix* it in time one again.

Here the question arises what we could have done? To begin with, after the knowledge acquired in 2003 from SARS-CoV, we could have been ready with antiviral drugs that could have prevented a broad range of bat SARS-like CoVs. We knew that there's one protein present in the genome of these viruses – the RNA dependent RNA polymerase. This is essential for the creation of all viral RNAs – is the most highly preserved protein, among all of these viruses. The task could have been to take a sample of these RdRps from bat CoVs, create them in cell culture, and locate small molecule compounds that inhibit all of them. We could have been ready with a pan-CoV antiviral drug developed with phase-I trials through human. We could have stockpiled for the next pandemic. However, it was a low priority, and hence there was no money to support such work. We failed to *Fix* it.

If it started at the right time, it might have even been possible to make a pan-CoV vaccine. At the same time, this would be much tougher and less assured than a pan-CoV antiviral treatment. There exists an approach on how the universal influenza vaccines are made. Preserved epitopes (the amino acids to which antibodies are directed) are identified on the viral spike protein. It would have been easy upfront to examine the spike proteins of many bat SARS-like CoVs. This identification for such conserved epitopes would have been much easier to design vaccines to foil them or manufacture monoclonal antibodies against such objects to be used medicinally. We failed to *Fix* it.

Today all of this research and more is taking place post mortem – too late to affect the pandemic. Today pharma companies worldwide, including India, are motivated because the profit is clearly visible. Until we reach for the available therapies – while it's too late to impact the 2020 outbreak – we are experimenting with drugs that were developed for other antiviral purposes. And they are clearly not ideal. Amongst the highly flaunted ones are Remdesivir and Favipiravir, the drugs that are to be given intravenously (it is not sufficiently absorbed after oral administration), this means it is typically given only to very sick patients. By that time, these drugs are administered, virus loads in the lung are already low, and giving an antiviral drug will have little impact. Surely, we could have had so much more than this. We failed to *Fix* it.

How have this preparation of this research crushed the SARS-CoV-2 pandemic? In one possible scenario, we have stockpiles of a pan-CoV antiviral drug. This would have been enough to treat millions of people. Back in late 2019 when SARS-CoV-2 was first identified in Wuhan, the drug could have been used immediately for large phase II efficacy trial. With this approach, we target not only sick people but all their contacts and contacts of contacts. We also cover health care personnel for this. The drug will considerably drop virus levels in the lung, weakening transmission. This would have followed with a larger phase III trial, with even more participants. With that approach, we could have restricted within China. Even if it had spread outside China, the tracing with use of the antiviral would have stopped further spread. Today we know that this assumption is based upon extensive testing and contact tracing. The process is not sufficiently carried out in the world. This should put us to shame for not responding quickly enough. We failed to *Fix* it.

Blaming the bats (while the source is yet to be confirmed) for accidentally giving humanity SARS-CoV-2, is easy. Who would blame both big pharma and the governments' world over for not coming up with a pan-CoV antiviral or vaccine? Big Pharma, the key player for being blind to anything that doesn't boost their bottom line. And the governments for under-funding so that critical research could not even be done in educational laboratories. Governments always fail to *Observe* for funding something for research on a virus that doesn't become a big mankind issue. We must end that scenario. We failed to *Fix* it.

Back in 2014, a research moratorium on certain kinds of this research was imposed due to coercion from various individuals who felt that establishing the pandemic potential of SARS-like CoV in bats was too perilous. One hopes that those authorities who triggered that moratorium feel at least a small amount of remorse when today they look at the raging impact of COVID-19 pandemic. Nature is not bound by our moratoriums. We failed to *Fix* it.

Today millions of people have died, economies worldwide have been destroyed. The social structure of the world has changed. Today the world is spending trillions on revival assistance. Just imagine how far cheaper prevention would have been if we could have just spent millions and saved the billions of dollars, millions of lives and crashed economies. We failed to *Fix* it.

One only hopes that the lesson learnt with this pandemic would at least improve government support for research on viruses. Those innocent viruses that are currently not harming humans, but have the potential to do so. That support would require from those in governments who release the money to look afar politics. The relationship with humans and viruses is not going away soon as humans continue to infringe upon the animal kingdom. Economic and political compulsions would always impact such research. Hence the question remains Will, anyone, ever *Fix* it or we will continue to learn the lessons penny wise pound foolishly.

Simply accepting reality and understanding your role in creating your circumstances will achieve little if you do not take action, solving real problems, and removing real obstacles on your road to results. To do so, you must exercise wisdom to *Fix*.

REACHING THE THIRD STEP ON WORKING CLOCK - *FIX*

In the corporate world, the challenge to *Fix* it is almost similar to that of Krishna convincing Arjun to take action on the battlefield. When one is out of the victim cycle, it is important to regularly ask "what extra I can do towards achieving my goals?" If you keep asking this question, you will avoid getting slipped into the victim cycle. You have to be mindful that getting on *Working Clock* is a process and not a single step. While on the journey, you have to continuously get over the hurdles and commit yourself towards your goal. Whenever you feel down, ask yourself the same question "what extra I can do towards achieving my goals?" Post-industrial era, the world moved towards the service industry and India is no exception. India emerged as the service centre for services for the world. Young, ambitious, English speaking manpower took over the "call centre" industry or ITES, Information Technology Enabled Services.

EMPLOYEE ENGAGEMENT CONNECTION

While the change happened from industrial worker to service provider, it brought its own set of challenges. Employee engagement issues were seldom heard in the industrial age. Most employees almost emulated machine functioning. They were expected to do a specific task at a specific time, and rest will be managed by others. Hence the expectations from both ends were clearly defined. The service industry hired young, aspirational people. They had a far better understanding of the world, thanks to the internet. India became the country offering the cheapest internet rates. Almost everyone from blue-collar to white-collar has mobiles that are connected to the world 24x7. They are up to date about whatever is happening in the world and their country, industry, company, and practically about everything. So, the challenge, managers started to face is how we keep this workforce productively engaged. Companies worldwide are questioning the efficacy of annual appraisal systems. Annual appraisal systems based upon bell curve perhaps lost their efficacy in the digitally connected world. Today people are used to "Likes" and Emoji's to express and not a numerical rating. This new phenomenon is changing the way traditional companies are *Fixed*.

More than a quarter of employees are at a high risk of turnover. What's worse is that one-third of those at high risk for turnover are talented, motivated employees who exceed performance expectations. They can easily find other positions, and they know it.

Research by Glassdoor in 2018 reported that 53% of employees are confident that if they quit or lost their current job, they would be able to find a comparable position within six months. To us, this trend indicates one thing: If you don't give employees a compelling reason to stay, they'll find another job that does. When competition for top talent is fierce, and the cost of training new hires is steep, you can't afford to not engage your employees, especially when you consider the corollary benefits of innovation, higher profits, and the sheer enjoyment of standing at the helm of a fully engaged workforce.

Let's address what is Employee Engagement first. **Engagement is the ability to be present, focused, and energised. But what it does is even more interesting. Engaged people go around moving clockwise towards *Working Clock*. They continue to progress because they feel part of a purpose larger than themselves. The purpose is the foundation of engagement – it's the vital element that makes an engaged organisation possible and the first step to creating an engaged culture that leads everyone towards *Working Clock*.**

5 STEPS TO INCREASING THE ENGAGEMENT QUOTIENT

How do you make the entire organisation, that's less dependent on machines move to *Working Clock* with the highest engagement? Following are the five steps you can follow to make employees far more Engaged and help *Fix* while moving to *Working Clock*.

1. **Connect your people to an Engaged Purpose that is written for them and is quite engaging.** The engaged purpose is a written statement that communicates to your team what your company does, who for, and why. This sets the tone to *Fix* attitude leading towards *Working Clock*. A lot of purposes, missions, or vision statements are written, not for employees – they are always written for the shareholders or customers. Like Mr Vineet Nayar (ex CEO HCL Technology) says Employee First, Customer Second as once you have an engaged employee, engaged customers naturally follow.

2. **Engagement should be regularly measured. In many companies**, HR will send out an employee engagement survey once a year. This method provides employee feedback only to capture their mood at that time of the year, rather than providing a helpful picture of engagement throughout the year. Demonstrate the *Fix* it behaviours regularly and motivate employees to follow.

3. **Stakeholders must demonstrate that engagement is not just a passing trend but a permanent focus.** Stakeholders must be clear that employee engagement is to support their well-being. They have to make sure that the engagement is true and honest and not just a check in the box. The *Fix* it attitude and behaviour takes time to inculcate.

4. **Listen to your team on their terms**, let them speak out the way they prefer. Let them have a safe environment and mechanism for enabling them to provide their feelings and feedback with confidentially. They will provide their honest views and not just what they think you want to hear. If employees are confident that that engagement is important to you, they will open up with ideas. They are the champions to suggest how to *Fix* it.

5. **Take action on feedback.** After your team has provided you with the feedback, ensure to use that feedback or survey report to action some simple things immediately. This would strengthen their confidence. You need to demonstrate your willingness to *Fix* it. This will provide you with the momentum you need to go after the longer-term behavioural change. Like we saw in Japanese fans example, who cleaned their area of the stadium despite their team losing out in qualifying match of the world cup.

OWN

In moving the organisation to *Working Clock* model, it is critical to change the way people view their responsibility and *Accountability*. Change of any kind is a struggle with fear, anger, and uncertainty, a war against old habits, hide-bound thinking, and entrenched interests. No company can change any faster than it can change the hearts and minds of its people. The key to change is to get people thinking differently about their jobs and their *Accountability*; to get them to see that they "could."

CASE STUDY : ROYAL ENFIELD (RE)

> *"When the going gets tough, the tough get going. We have not had negative growth in a decade. It's (fall in sales) a blip... The RE story is very much intact."*
>
> *~Siddhartha Lal, Managing Director, Eicher Motors*

Every Wednesday the ritual starts at 9 am. A large building of about 18,000 square feet on the National Highway number 2 in Uttar Pradesh (UP) is filled with an exuberant bunch of young and passionate 'devotees' from the nearby village of Maholi. The gathering also includes over a dozen turbaned middle-aged men in their early 40s who have come for a glimpse of the main 'deities' enshrined at Aryaman Enterprises. A dealership around 2 kilometres away from Mathura, the temple city. The tittle-tattle ebbs suddenly as Krishna Singh enters the sprawling edifice. The bulky 'priest', dressed in a brown leather jacket with armour pockets on its shoulders, appears and greets the crowd while walking towards the sanctum sanctorum. This is where an aesthetically designed Classic-350 is mounted on a wooden platform. Singh, a young 28 year, while glancing at his Apple watch lowers his Ray-Ban glasses. At the turn of 9 am, he starts the machine by pressing the electric start button and goes on to rev up to full acceleration with a twist of the wrist.

Standing atop a fleet of Bullets and Thunderbirds he says that the thrill of the throttle can only be understood by these 'devotees'. This makes other followers follow the ritual.

Singh tells us that "this showroom is a temple for us". They opened it in 2015 when just 6-7 per cent of all bikes bought were financed. Nowadays, about 60 per cent are bought on finance at Aryaman.

He flagged off another outlet about 45 kilometres from Mathura at Kosi Kalan a couple of years ago. "Royal Enfield bikes have a cult-like following in UP," he contends. From 2015 to 2019 the sales had spiked from 25 bikes per month to 170 units in March 2019. This has made UP become the second biggest market for RE in volumes.

The sales have been gradually falling at the start of the year 2019. 7, 14 and 20 per cent was the fall respectively in the first three months of the year. Product fatigue contributed to de-growth. Eicher Motors, Royal Enfield's Classic 350 is the highest-selling model, and it has not had an upgrade or variant in last decade since its launch.

However, Siddhartha Lal, MD at Eicher Motors, which manufactures Royal Enfield motorcycles is not pressing the alarm button. He quotes "It's not normal, but equally not alarming". The RE story is about the premium segment, and it's strongly in place," says Lal. In 2019 early April, Lal came up with a fundamental shift in the way Eicher Motors will be managed. He appointed Vinod Dasari as a CEO to be at the helm of the day-to-day running of RE's domestic operation. Lal, himself London-based freed up himself to execute a larger play including international expansion.

Lal wrote to his employees "To achieve our audacious goal of 2030, to catalyse and reshape the world of motorcycling towards middle-weights (350-750cc), thereby growing at twice the pace of the industry, we need to run the company differently". He further added that "I believe I can serve RE better by playing a role that is different from the CEO." Dasari is the man Lal is counting on to grow RE to the next growth phase. Dasari is also appointed as an Executive Director with a berth on Eicher Motors board.

Royal Enfield started recovery with the launch of Classic 350 from 2010 onwards. This model still makes for over 70 per cent of sales of RE. Lal followed a series of radical top-down steps that made possible for Classic 350 in achieving cult status. A radical top-down marketing approach Lal followed was to make seven top cities Delhi, Mumbai, Bengaluru, Chennai, Kolkata, Pune, and Hyderabad as catchment areas for consumers to visit from smaller places. He explained that Punjab & Kerala were already doing well for them. The idea of making big seven cities as hubs were to provide a 'wow' experience to consumers. Handpicked dealers were selected, stores revamped, and employees educated. If a guy from Kanpur, Lal explains, comes to Delhi and visits the store, he should go back with the feeling of desire to buy the motorcycle. "It was a trickle-down effect," he says. Along with new-look stores, RE began organising rides and hosting events for its users, which helped it 'pull' users towards the brand.

The same year the pull strategy was adeptly supported by with the expansion of dealer network across India. They added about 100 dealers every year for seven years from 2011 to 2018. Followed by the expansion in big cities, the focus shifted to smaller towns. They soon realised the importance of financing that hugely helped in the speedy uptick and critical for growth. High resale value was another reason for quick acceptance with finance options.

There were exclusive teams deployed to work with financiers both at the corporate and regional level. The manufacturer also sourced back motorcycles from users. With high ticket price, good residual value, very good customers, and the lowest delinquency in the industry it was a win-win for financiers.

The growth was supported by another trend, that started around 2011 but picked up pace over the next few years, that was the improvisation of RE bikes. Premiumization also helped alongside, with customers upgrading from 350cc plus segment. The price in this category was upward of Rs 1.65 lakh.

The first set of aspirational commuters were those who were upgrading from 150, 180, or 200cc, back in 2011. Four years later, the second stage of the upgrade started. Many 100cc users started buying RE. The third stage of upgrade started happening around late 2018. RE became the choice of aspirational first time buying youngsters. First time RE buyers rose to about a sixth of total RE customers. The trend also helped in the faster pace of migration from the customer segment in 100-180cc to the premium above 250cc segment.

The premium segment is likely to outpace the average segment over the next decade, as per Lal's prediction. However, Covid-19 impacted demand for every player in the automobile industry.

Lal is a long term player. He says that if an investor is looking at quarterly numbers to stay relevant, they should quit and sell it to someone with long term view. He is not greedy for the short-term gains. He says this short-term thinking circuit is not there in my brain.

Now, the RE story has taken a hit owing to the pandemic as its recent numbers are 44% lower compared to last year. In contrast, the numbers were on a growth trajectory before the pandemic hit India. The question here is not about what will happen to the RE story. The learning here is that the company had the *Fix* it attitude deep-rooted in their DNA. They did not bend with the pressure of dropping sales. They did not question the product acceptance. They rather focussed on how to grow.

WHAT IF YOU DON'T *FIX* IT

As our next case demonstrates, it's not uncommon for people to *Observe, Own,* and then fail to *Fix.*

At Cuckoobird, an automobile component company (name disguised to protect the privacy of one of our clients), two promoters had come to their wits' end dealing with their two directors. The director of marketing and the director of operations. Director Marketing would not fully accept responsibility for meeting product launch deadlines and the right communication standards. While intelligent and competent, he would just not be systematic. When the deadline approached, he would offer some or the other reason for not being ready yet. On the other hand, the other directors, responsible for different areas, saw the reality of the situation clearly and even Owned their circumstances, but they could not move forward to *Fix.* They had become stuck in their inability to move beyond the *Own* it step. Their attitude of "we can't intervene in other's work" extracted their willingness to ask how to *Fix* question. While everyone responsible around could *Observe* and *Own* but they dropped like a *Stuck Clock* in failing to *Fix.* Their mind-sets made a successful company in the industry into an also-ran player.

In a similar example, another company that is the leader in wires and switchgear failed to *Fix.* While the promoter hired a very senior strategy professional from one of the global consulting companies, even he could not *Fix* the situation. When we interacted with people there, we realised that all stakeholders could *Observe* and *Own* but are helpless to *Fix* since the decision rests with the Chairman. For reasons unknown to stakeholders, the company could be on the way towards falling like a *Stuck Clock.* Older people in the company rue what they could have achieved, considering the brand value company enjoyed for decades. New players with lower quality could trample this company since it lacked the willingness to *Fix*. In our consulting experience, we have seen that many companies can *Observe* the ensuing trouble. They also have an attitude to *Own* the situation. However, their inability to *Fix* the situation pushes the company towards *Stuck Clock* situation. Once the company goes into a *Stuck Clock* situation, it becomes more and more difficult to *Fix* and move it like *Working Clock*, and they remain a subject of case studies of famous failures.

TOP 10 SKILLS TO *FIX* A STUCK CLOCK

Let us look at the 10 most important skills required to *Fix* the situation leaning towards *Stuck Clock*:

1. **Self-starter:** Everyone on the team has to be a self-starter, and you are leading it. You have to be surrounded by smart self-starters, even if they don't agree with you. Usually, self-starters won't need much coaching or encouragement to move forward.

2. **Team players:** Everyone has to pull together. You can have spirited dialogue, but you can't have arguments. Fly like a group of birds who keep changing their position of leadership.

3. **Customer service:** You can't afford to compromise on customer service. Imagine the situation where you spend huge money on promotions, but when customers call to enquire, there's nobody to answer. That's not reassuring.

4. **Take responsibility:** If things don't work, admit your mistake and move on. Don't linger and beat yourself up. Everyone has a right to be wrong, once.

5. **New ideas:** Start looking for and soliciting new ideas that will breathe life into the business. It will show everyone you're alive and focused on the future. Pick a few you can afford and implement them.

6. **Take a pay cut:** Industry leaders who are open to take a pay-cut or forego their entire salary sends a very strong intent signal. This move reassures people that you aren't giving up yet and ready to fight.

7. **Never blame the soldier:** Defence services in India are known to lead by example, if something goes wrong, instead of finding a scapegoat, officers own it up.

8. **Compromise:** Not your integrity or principles but your approach. You may have been known for the best company for payments but during tough times, compromise and negotiate with your partners for the better payment term. Explain to them the situation, and most likely they would agree.

9. **Ears to the ground:** You must ensure that you are someone people don't think to approach. You appreciate that anyone, despite hierarchy, may have a suggestion and you welcome it.

10. **Optimistic:** This has to be the underlying behaviour of yours. If you demonstrate shakiness or pessimism, it is unlikely that people will follow you.

ACCOUNTABILITY SKILL QUIZ

To assess whether, and to what extent, you practice these skills and competencies, you can complete the following *Fix* attitude Self-assessment. Evaluate each of the skills by determining whether your attitudes and behaviours always, never, or sometimes show evidence of them:

Mark yourself on each skill that best demonstrates your attitude and behaviours:

1. **Self-starter:** You are the one who starts to roll up the sleeves of your shirt?
   Mostly Sometimes Seldom
   3   2   1

2. **Team player:** You don't blink an eye to pass the baton for team progression?
   Mostly Sometimes Seldom
   3   2   1

3. **Customer service:** You truly believe in the concept that a complaint is a gift?
   Mostly Sometimes Seldom
   3   2   1

4. **Take responsibility:** You don't wait for things to become obvious and then take responsibility?
   Mostly Sometimes Seldom
   3   2   1

5. **New ideas:** You are a magnet for new ideas and qualify them quickly to implement?
   Mostly Sometimes Seldom
   3   2   1

6. **Take a pay cut**: You are ever ready to contribute to the bottom line?

   Mostly Sometimes Seldom

   3   2   1

7. **Blame the soldier:** You look for people around to pin the blame?

   Mostly Sometimes Seldom

   3   2   1

8. **Compromise:** You respect the value of cash and compromise your system to reserve?

   Mostly Sometimes Seldom

   3   2   1

9. **Ears to the ground:** You make sure to visit the last soldier on the border?

   Mostly Sometimes Seldom

   3   2   1

10. **Optimistic:** Come what may, you do not have the word failure in your dictionary?

    Mostly Sometimes Seldom

    3   2   1

Now, let's evaluate to see where you stand when it comes to *Fix* attitude. Add up your scores on all the above ten statements basis your selection.

30-20 Indicates that you appreciate your *Accountability* and own the circumstances. You do possess a *Fix*ing attitude. Great show!

19-10 Means you are on an average scale, meaning you oscillate between *Fix*ing or letting go. You need to work harder to stay on *Working Clock*.

9-1 Indicates that you are still on *Stuck Clock*. You feel that it's not you someone else needs to *Fix*.

KEY TAKEAWAY

Understanding this third step to *Fix*, you take greater *Accountability* that will enhance your skills to solve problems and remove the bottlenecks you encounter as you progress on your path towards *Working Clock*. "What else can we do to rise above our circumstances and get the results we want?"

By discussing this question, often you air your concerns that become the starting step towards a *Fix*ing attitude. Siddhartha Lal of RE did not give up on the optimism. He knew that his fundamentals are right, and he need not worry. He knew that for expansion, he needs a full-time CEO so that he can focus on expansion and exports. Market conditions did not change his fundamental *Fix*ing, attitude. He did sulk looking at one of the largest competitors going down. He knew that if a customer likes his product, he can *Fix* other things around.

Each journey towards *Working Clock* is fraught with attitudes and behaviours that make people optimistic. The journey is never over. Siddhartha Lal or any other optimistic leader in all their plans would have never anticipated the onslaught of the Covid19 pandemic, taking away virtually a year of business growth, negative cash flows, migrant labour issues, squeeze on the line of credit, virtually zero demand for over a quarter, a pile-up of inventory, huge debtors issues, everything that makes businesses grow. But, people like Siddhartha Lal are not going to give up or be pessimistic. They know that however big this jolt is, eventually they will grow. They are a true believer that languishing in *Stuck Clock* will only make them redundant.

CHAPTER

7

Repeat

pāpam evāśrayed asmān
hatvaitān ātatāyina
tasmān nārhā vaya hantu
dhārtarārān sa-bāndhavān
sva-jana hi katha hatvā
sukhina syāma mādhava

"Sin will overcome us if we slay such aggressors. Therefore
it is not proper for us to kill the sons of Dhtarāra and our
friends. What should we gain,
O Kiha, husband of the goddess of fortune, and how could
we be happy by killing our own kinsmen?"

LESSONS FROM MAHABHARATA

Arjun tried every bit to avoid war and thus avoid responsibility.
But Krishna kept reminding him of how it would not be Dharma
for a Kshatriya (warrior) if he ditches his prime responsibility.
He has to take this battle to its logical end, failing which, Krishna
has to break his vow to not use the weapons.

The situation in companies is not too different; those who are
pushing towards *Working Clock* are often challenged by those on
the other side. For every one person trying to *Repeat* the solutions
learnt in the *Fix* stage, there are 10 against him. Hence, this step
becomes so crucial in ensuring that all efforts are made to come
to *Fix* state cannot be frittered away if they are not Repeated.

CASE STUDY : NAUKRI.COM

A business mind always thinks about the opportunities behind the problems & finds the solution for it. Entrepreneurship is something that comes with passion. And you can see that passion in an entrepreneur from the beginning, just like Sanjeev Bikhchandani; founder of India's largest job posting portal Naukri.com. At the age of 12, when most of the kids worry about new games & toys, Sanjeev decided that he will become an entrepreneur. At that stage, the idea started forming in his head that, somewhere along the way, he would be starting a company of his own. Not only Naukri.com, but Sanjeev also founded two more companies, i.e. Infoedge Pvt. Ltd & Indmark. Sanjeev Bikhchandani did his schooling at St. Columbia School, Delhi, and passed out in 1980. He completed his graduation in B. A. (Economics) from St. Stephen's College, DU. After graduation, he decided to go for a job for two years, before starting his own business. So he opted for a marketing job at HMM (now known as GlaxoSmithKline) selling Horlicks and within a year and a half, quit that comfortable marketing job to start his own business.

While at the IT Asia Exhibition in New Delhi, in October 1996, Sanjeev Bikhchandani stumbled upon the "WWW" as a heading of stall signage. Curious, he wondered. He has been searching for trademarks for big pharmaceutical companies over the past few years. He has also been doing salary surveys for companies. This perhaps was the Eureka moment for him. WWW galvanised his curiosity. When he enquired from the stall owner about it, he was told it means "World Wide Web". This moment Sanjeev was exposed to the internet. The promoter at the stall further explained about Yahoo! website. He showed Sanjeev how to browse, search, and find out about other sites. When

Sanjeev enquired about how many people in India are internet users, he was told "Fourteen thousand". Sanjeev told himself, "Wow! That's a lot of people". Sanjeev's brother was a professor at UCLA business school, so he called him to understand more and expressed his desire to get onto the internet. He wanted to start with a website and hire a server for him. For the server fee, Sanjeev offered his brother five per cent in the website he called Info Edge. Info Edge is the same company that got listed on bourses having a market capitalisation of Rupees Fifteen Thousand Crores (about $2.3 billion). For sure his brother got a great deal for investing 5 per cent or Rupees one thousand ($25), a month back then for the server.

Without the complete knowledge of Sanjeev, on the unexplored path a few years later, Info Edge started to take the shape of a business that could become a gold mine for Sanjeev. It was the year 1997 when Sanjeev launched Naukri.com, an Indian job portal as a subsidiary of Info Edge. After reaching extraordinary heights in the United States in 1998, the dot com bubble arrived in India in 1998. Around 1999, Sanjeev started with his first round of luck, in 1999 he started receiving calls from investors to invest in his business. Sanjeev recalls how he was completely baffled as he had no idea about the dot com bubble, valuation or venture capital. In 1999 Info Edge made about Rs.36 lakh (roughly about $51 thousand) in revenues.

He was happy as the things were moving fine. He never thought of raising any external capital. He recalls for the inquisitiveness, he went for a couple of meetings. He refused to accept any outside investment as he knew building the business brick by brick, pay as you go by earning revenues and managing every dime as if it was a dollar was the way to go.

However, having witnessed the frenzy over the two decades, he has seen three cycles of investment. The first one happened in 1999, the next one in 2008, and then in 2014. It's not easy to hold back, quips Sanjeev as an internet entrepreneur and angel investor. It is confusing half of the time to wonder, "What is it that others have realised, but I haven't?". A few months later, JobsAhead.com was launched as a competition. Their launch advertising budget was Rupees Seventy Five Lakh (about a hundred thousand dollars), double the turnover of Info Edge's annual turnover.

By the end of 2000, Sanjeev and his team decided to take the plunge and raised about Rupees Seven Crores ($1.7 million) from ICICI ventures. However, the dot-com meltdown started about four months later in March 2001. Over the next six months, there was no official acknowledgement. Everybody maintained that it's a technical correction. Sanjeev and his team kept the funding that was received from ICICI ventures in April in *Fix*ed deposit.

Having three years' experience in the world of internet, they knew how difficult it was to survive. They knew that the market crash is for real. They convinced ICICI that the crash is real and the business has to be built slowly. JobsAhead.com, on the other hand, was launched with big fanfare and created a buzz. It had better user experience and was "good looking" compared to Naukri.com. However, Sanjeev and his team kept the money in the bank FD instead of matching up with the competition. JobsAhead.com gave good competition for some time to Naukri.com.

They had raised about Rupees eleven crores (about $1.5 million) over three rounds. Their last round was valued around Rs. Thirty-three crores (about $4.5 millions). JobsAhead.com continued to grow with aggressive sales and marketing techniques. While the internet bust recovery was happening slowly, 9/11 happened in the US. This resulted in further pressure on the job market in India like all over the world. JobsAhead continued to expand in a hurry while Sanjeev and his team were going slow to build profits.

At that time, Sanjeev hired four salespeople in Delhi to meet prospective clients and make sales. They soon realised that a good salesperson would not only pay for himself but also make a profit for the company. Sanjeev acknowledges that four salespeople who were hired started actually contributing to the bottom-line and adding about rupees one lakh and twelve thousand per month net. That provided a repeatable business model, and Naukri kept adding more salespeople. Amongst many things that helped Naukri were, brand traction, the right strategy and the most jobs on its portal.

We had insider knowledge and learning curves that helped us. When 9/11 hit, JobsAhead.com realised that their last round of Rs 11 crores funding would need to last a very long time, so they started laying off employees. And a lot of these well-trained people ended up at Naukri.com, further fuelling our machine. After booking losses for two years, Naukri.com not only broke even but also made a profit of rupees one crore (about $135 thousand). The journey was quite a challenge for Naukri.com, as the competition, while entering late was beating them in their own game. Finally, in 2002, Naukri.com launched resume database two years after JobsAhead and five years after their website launch.

Eventually, Naukri.com could beat its competitor despite Monster.com's acquisition of JobsAhead.com in 2004 Naukri. com was still getting more traffic on their site. Sanjeev recalls how they almost didn't make it. He shares a valuable lesson of keeping a track on competitor while treating your customer better than the competition.

Stopping at three steps of *Observe, Own* and *Fix* may still leave you exposed to dangers and threats of the environment. You have to learn how to *Repeat* and keep enhancing your game. Every challenge becomes your learning and gets added to your experience to *Repeat.*

Sanjeev did not rest at any step. When his job site was at the peak, numero-uno was its status; he ensured that he kept going back to *Observe, Own* and *Fix.* During one of my visits to a small city during my official trip, I was chatting up with the Sales Manager to understand how are we doing in the market and what better can be done? I was with Monster.com at that time. He told me that "we are a big company, but we can't do what Sanjeev does as 'promoter', he would arrive by the first flight in the city without informing anyone.

He would straight go to a few customers who have Naukri.com's subscription and take their feedback as a potential subscriber. After that, he would pillion ride on a two-wheeler with a seller to visit some subscribers of Naukri.com and understand by chatting up with sellers as to what are the typical problems they face while selling.

Ultimately, personal *Accountability,* like Sanjeev, means accepting full responsibility for results. It requires the sort of attitude Sanjeev demonstrated to build one of the first and biggest e-commerce brands in India. Failing to accept full responsibility will always deprive you of reaping the most valuable benefit that is derived from full *Accountability.* Taking full responsibility by overcoming your circumstances and achieving the results you want is the obvious benefits one reaps. While many benefits that accrue from applying the first three steps results only come when you put all four steps together and *Repeat!*

CASE STUDY : MAHINDRA HOLIDAYS

Another renowned leader of the Indian corporate sector Arun Nanda who is the current Chairman of Mahindra Lifespaces and Executive Director MHRIL (Mahindra Holidays and Resorts India). He is known for his fierce eye on consumer services. One of the resort managers during my visit to their resorts in the hills of North India shared a story about Arun Nanda. After arriving in the resort, he would straight head to check the rooms.

He would go to his room in the end after he checked all unoccupied rooms, kitchen, play area, and all facilities. When enquired, the resort manager said that he prefers to call the resort as his own and would rather keep it the way he would keep it for his family and guests. This is how Arun would ensure all four steps of the *Working Clock* are implemented. Mahindra Group has adopted a philosophy of Rise in everything they do. This philosophy is connected to the steps we are discussing in *Working Clock*. Mahindra Group's 2018 turnover stood at Rs.105806 Crores (USD 20.07 Billion).

FUTURE FOCUS

The big difference in *Repeat* step from the earlier three steps is the future focus. This step ensures the successes achieved in the previous steps of Observe, Own, and Fix is *Repeated*. Like Dr Stephen Covey lays importance about the 7th Habit in his book *7 Habits of Highly Effective People.* He says that after learning and practising the previous six habits, one has to ensure that the 7th Habit of continuous learning becomes part of your professional journey.

Repeat step would ensure that you are not only practising what you have learned in the previous three steps but also keep repeating to learn about the future preventive actions.

This not only benefits you personally, but it also leaves a huge positive impact on the company. This success comes after you have progressed through all four steps towards *Working Clock*. If you fail to *Repeat*, you increase your chances of falling towards *Stuck Clock*.

Like we have been consistently saying that *Accountability* is a process and not one giant step. Your continuous efforts in following all four steps will ensure that you do not get into the victim mode ever.

Any form of *Accountability* is fraught with risk, but we never said that owning *Accountability* is easy. If you continuously follow the required steps, the chances of you falling into the victim mode are minimum.

Fear of risk outcomes make many people avoid *Repeat* step. They get tired of continuously doing the four steps again and again. They feel that if they have achieved success until three steps, then it's okay to leave at the *Fix* step, they run the risk of becoming a victim again in the absence of the *Repeat* approach.

Just like Owning, the second step of *Accountability* is so logical after Observing, Repeating is so logical after learning *Fix*ing with the earlier two steps.

CASE STUDY : ZAPPOS STORY

Consider the example of Zappos as Claus Moller and Janelle Barlow captured in their book 'A Complaint is A Gift'. Zappos did not train its customer support executives to sell shoes, but they trained them to solve their problems. They did not stop at the *Fix* step, rather they made all three steps of *Observe, Own*, and *Fix* so nicely integrated into *Repeat* that customer service became a culture. One of their executive in the middle of the night understood that their customer is hungry and likes to have a pizza.

The luxury hotel he is staying in has refused to make pizza since they have a closed their kitchen and can serve only sandwiches. Zappos customer facing executive could have politely refused, as they are a shoe selling company. But, the *Repeat* step was part of their culture. She went out of her way to locate a nearby pizzeria and order pizza to be delivered to the guest. She also requested the guest that he has to come to the reception of his hotel lobby since the pizza delivery boy will not be allowed to serve inside the hotel.

During my various travels related to work, I used to stay in particular properties at different locations. Most of the staff members were familiar, owing to my fortnightly trips. One such property called Maya Palace is located in city beautiful, Chandigarh Sector-35. I used to stay in that hotel for a few reasons, while it wasn't the best in the city. My office was walkable compared to better hotels where I would need to hire a car. Hygiene wise it was amongst the best in its peers. But the most important reason was the service. During one of the trips, I came back late from work, around 11.15 at night, at the hotel reception. Collected the key and headed straight to the room. Within five minutes, I received a call from reception "sir would you like to have dinner?" I knew that their kitchen would be closed by now, so I said: "No, thank you. My stomach is not in the best shape and tomorrow morning I will have to rush early, so let me skip the dinner, and anyway it's late". The person on the other end politely said thank you and kept the phone.

After about 5 minutes, I received a call from Rajesh, the Asst. Manager front office. He asked me "sir, would you like to have khichdi (a paste-like dish made with rice and lentils)?" I was surprised since no hotel menu has khichdi in it, and Rajesh also knows that it's good for an upset stomach. So I enquired, "Rajesh are you still in the property?"

He said "no, but before leaving, I had asked my colleague to check with you for dinner. So, he told me that you are not feeling great, so I thought of checking with you" I said, "no, I think it's late for your kitchen to make it now, I'd rather have fruit salad and medicine to sleep". He said, "Sir it's our job to take care of you, no problems, you will get khichdi in fifteen minutes". After that, he also added, "sir would you like to have curd-rice in the breakfast in case your stomach is still not perfect?" I was overwhelmed by the service. This mid-range hotel, being in north India, would typically not have either of these preparations. But here's someone willing to go the extra mile for customer delight.

Rajesh did not follow the typical customer service and like the Zappos executive went out of his way to serve their customer. These two examples show us the benefits of the *Repeat* step. A couple of years later, I was informed that the same hotel had opened another star hotel The Maya, in Jalandhar (Punjab) and they just enquired about my next travel date and sent me a booking confirmation in the different city in their hotel. People and organisations who follow all the four steps of *Accountability*, while staying on *Working Clock*, also influence others near them.

REPEATING : WHAT STOPS PEOPLE?

Most people naturally resist the perceived risks associated with becoming fully responsible for results. Those who fail to *Repeat* or *Fix*, can't or won't resist the pull from *Stuck Clock* which can easily drag someone back into the victim cycle. This would lead to wasting valuable time, energy, and resources, ignoring and denying, making excuses, giving explanations, raising fingers, creating confusion, and waiting to see if things will get better.

Taking the final step to *Accountability* becomes virtually impossible as the fear of failure can create a terrible burden. It's easier for people to hide in a false sense of security, giving excuses for inaction. A risk-avoiding attitude will surely keep you in the victim cycle. This is applicable at organisation levels as well. Successful organisations embrace the risk associated with action, despite the perceived dangers associated with that action. Steps on *Working Clock* truly separates great companies from good ones.

When companies decide to move towards *Working Clock*, they equip their employees with risk-taking appetite. Those companies understood the risks involved and perceived benefits in extending that option.

In case the companies fail to provide that platform of taking risks and trying something new, employees anyway venture out to pursue their passions. Progressive companies initiate steps to make people shift towards *Working Clock*, with or without complete support from the employer.

CASE STUDY : SHORT CORPORATE LESSONS

3M CORPORATION

3M Corporation established a 15% project an initiative. When this program was established, the United States' workforce was composed of highly inflexible employment opportunities in rigid business structures. 3M developed an ethos: Innovate or die right after WWII had ended. The original projects that came out of this initiative had widely successful outcomes. It resulted in Scientists developing and manufacturing products that remain utilised internationally, even decades later.

GOOGLE

Right from the start of the 21st century, the founders of Google have encouraged the 20% project system on similar lines of 15% 3M project. Additional five per cent compared to its predecessor, the increase in the time dedicated to projects triggered further growth in the company's levels.

Gmail is one such outcome of this initiative amongst many over the last twenty years. Taking a cue from this initiative, schools in the US have taken up and implemented a similar system for students within the classroom. This initiative helps students to experiment with ideas without fear of assessment and increases their involvement in their general studies and upgrade the creatively. There are many small businesses who started using this system in their day-to-day functions, including software company Atlassian, as a safeguard to counter damp growth rates and a general lack of innovation.

ENTREPRENEURSHIP LESSONS FROM INDIA

Serial entrepreneurs have proved how important it is to *Repeat* their business models to test. These entrepreneurs are continuously brimming with ideas, identifying pain points, and itching to build solutions. The journey of a start-up founder is innately "lonely". Many entrepreneurs use "lonely" word to tell their stories. They go through the highs that kiss the sky, but there are lows, more often than not, which can make founders slip into a deep, dark abysm of *Stuck Clock*. Some of them are able to manage to dodge them and continue successful run with their businesses - not once or twice but many more times. The reason they are called "Serial entrepreneurs", is because they continuously *Observe, Own, Fix* and *Repeat* with ideas, identifying pain points, and find solutions. A recent Forbes article notes: "Serial entrepreneurship is a calling.

Not many people know they're a serial entrepreneur until they have already become one." They are often willing to quit the cushy comforts of an established business and get themselves into the frying pan all over again. Many times over. India's had a few of them too. Those have gone on to set benchmarks in entrepreneurship over the years (2020 excluded).

MYNTRA

Myntra's founder Mukesh Bansal, India's most successful online fashion retailer, sold it to Flipkart in 2014 in what was then the largest e-commerce transaction (Rs 2,000 crore deal) in the country's start-up ecosystem. Bansal not only built a strong brand in Myntra, but he also created successful private labels business. This business continues to drive Flipkart's fashion sales. After selling Myntra, Bansal moved on to another idea, like most true-blue entrepreneurs. He took up a fresh challenge in 2016 and launched Cure.fit, a health and fitness start-up from Bengaluru. His plans include presence in 15 cities over four-five years. Another extension of Cure.fit was expansion into the mental wellness space with Mind.fit in the year 2017. Next year in October 2018 it spread into the QSR space with Eat.fit. The start-up is funded by other leading VCs like IDG Ventures, Accel Partners, and Kalaari Capital, among others.

TAXI FOR SURE

Aprameya Radhakrishna's entrepreneurship first venture saw him set up a taxi start-up for budget riders. He grew it to a 15,000-vehicle fleet before selling it to market leader Ola for $200 million in a cash-and-equity deal in 2015. Aprameya, an IIM-A alumnus, was deemed a success because he had "built and sold" his venture in 2015. Ola within a year of acquisition dissolved that brand into Ola. However, by then Aprameya as an active angel investor-backed about 12 start-ups, including Unacademy, DailyNinja, Goodbox, YourDost, etc. Aprameya is also launched his second entrepreneurial venture - Vokal, a peer-to-peer knowledge-sharing platform for India's regional language users. The start-up is funded by Accel Partners, Blume Ventures, and Shunwei Capital.

GOQII

Another serial entrepreneur Vishal Gondal way back in 1999 founded India Games. That was the time mobile internet was non-existent, and nobody had heard mobile gaming in India. Irrespective of that, he went on to build it into India's largest mobile gaming company before selling it to Disney twelve years later in 2011. He made $100 million from that deal. Like any other entrepreneur, Gondal too was restless and loved the "chaos" of entrepreneurship. So, three years later, he returned to the start-up space with his wearable tech venture - GOQii. He was able to rope in investors like California-headquartered start-up New Enterprise Associates (NEA), Edelweiss' VC arm, Vijay Shekhar Sharma, and Ratan Tata. Gondal's vision about GOQii is a holistic, subscription-based health and wellness solution that consists of a fitness band, a health coach, preventive health services, access to hospitals and diagnostic centres, and more.

CONTEST2WIN

Alok Kejriwal after Gondal is another leading entrepreneur in mobile gaming and digital space. Back in 1998, when the word "start-up" wasn't fashionable, Alok built Contests2Win. Contest2Win was India's first online contesting site. Tasting success in 2001, Alok launched a mobile-to-TV interactive platform, Mobile2Win and turned it into a huge success within four years. He was able to rope in partnering with multiple TV channels for reality shows. Like any other serial entrepreneur, Alok sold Mobile2win to Norwest Venture Partners. In 2007, he launched his most successful – start-up, Games2Win. It specialised in developing original mobile games and was a huge hit in the US market. It also ranked among the world's top 20 online gaming businesses. Alok is known for his ability to create value at minimal investments. At present, he mentors first-generation entrepreneurs and helps them connect with VC networks.

These four entrepreneurs establish the importance of *Repeat* success. When people find success in *Repeat*, they don't sit back and enjoy; instead, they keep Repeating all the steps on *Working Clock*. Not surprisingly, many people find it much easier to go with the status quo and allow themselves to be "acted upon" even when that behaviour gets them into trouble, rather than confront the risks that so often attend moving from *Fix*ing to Repeating. With a good deal more vigilance concerning the dangers of *Stuck Clock* behaviour, companies and individuals may learn how shunning the risks associated with action can prevent them from creating a better future. Like our four examples above not only show us the value of action but also Repeating it.

MAKING OF WORKING CLOCK FROM STUCK CLOCK

CASE STUDY : LESSONS FROM AMITABH BACHCHAN LIFE

Amitabh Bachchan or AB or BIG B needs no introduction; his charisma is unrivalled. He remembers, "in the year 2000, when the entire world was celebrating the new century, I was celebrating my disastrous fortune. There were no films, no money, no company, a million legal cases against and the tax authorities had put notice of recovery on my home,"

AB first became famous as Angry young man of Hindi cinema or Bollywood in the early 1970s. Since then he has come up as one of the most prominent figures in Indian cinema. To his credit, he has 36 Filmfare nominations, the most in any major category. AB has worked as a playback singer, film producer, and television presenter, and was an elected member of the Indian Parliament from 1984 to 1987. In 1999, BBC Online Poll, named Amitabh Bachchan the Superstar of the Millennium while keeping the likes of Alec Guinness and Marlon Brando behind him. Madame Tussaud's in June 2000, erected a wax statue in his honour making him the first living Asian with that honour.

We can't say that his life has been a bed of roses. He faced a major accident on the sets of Coolie movie in 1982 for which he underwent surgery in November 2005. At the age of 57 in the year 2000, he had a financial crisis when he almost lost all that he had. The financial crisis doesn't discriminate among people in any income bracket or line of work and can affect any of us at any time in our lives. This example is all about how he landed into the crisis and how like his reel life, he emerged a hero, fighting all odds, displaying the *Repeat* behaviour.

AB started Amitabh Bachchan Corporation Ltd. (ABCL) in 1995. The company for film production and event management. On the lines of Hollywood studios, this was a first attempt in India to evolve as a corporatised entertainment company. First major achievement happened very next year in 1996 when ABCL brought the Miss World Pageant to India. However, without proper planning and management control and in tearing hurry to expand, it seemed to have spread itself too thin. ABCL – was anything and everything to do with the entertainment business

– for e.g. making films, distributing them, sell the music of the film, manage the actors who act in films and also have an event management group to leverage on the actor's brand equity as well. Add to that, television production by selling television's commercial time.

The vision of the company made it move very fast. ABCL recruited 150 people, launched 15 films with cost per film ranging from Rs 3 to 8 crores, got distribution rights for Bombay and Bandit Queen – both of which were successful at the box office – got into music with Aby Baby, Diljale, Rakshak, Tere Mere Sapne, etc., and of course on the event side the Miss World Pageant & and the BPL Dandia.

Miss World 1996, the 46th Miss World pageant was the big starting point as it took place on November 23, 1996, in the city of Bangalore, India. There were a total of 88 contestants participating from all over the world to take part in the prestigious event. That night, Irene Skliva of Greece took home the Miss World title.

However, the same event invited protests from women's groups and ending with the Spastics Society publicly denouncing the company's inability to pay up its promised charity. That event threw up more fits than profits for ABCL's first attempt at event management. The Miss World international organisation billed $2 million in fees from the local event manager. Adding up all other costs, ABCL run up a bill of an estimated Rs.17.5 Crore (roughly $5 million). Modest estimates suggest ABCL's loss at about Rs 4 crore.

However, in the very first year, ABCL achieved its target turnover of Rs 65 crore while making a profit of Rs 15 crores. The second-year was not so kind with that kind of growth. Amitabh Bachchan faced upset professional managers when Amitabh agreed to do stage shows in North America.

The professional managers grudged that the booking was not made through ABCL. The impasse finally resulted in a change of the top team. But the conditions did not improve. Its productions like Mrityudaata failed dismally at the boxoffice. By 1999 ABCL was facing an unprecedented liquidity crunch. Substantial funds were blocked in the distribution of films and production; staff salaries were delayed taking the public confidence to rock-bottom. In March 1999, ABCL approached the Board of Industrial and Financial Reconstruction to seek protection under the bankruptcy laws as it was hounded by creditors led by India's public broadcaster Doordarshan and Canara Bank.

Amitabh Bachchan's Mumbai bungalow 'Prateeksha 'and two flats were restrained by the Bombay High Court from selling off till the pending loan recovery cases of Canara Bank were dealt with. However, Bachchan pleaded that Sahara India Finance already has his bunglow papers as collateral for raising funds for ABCL. Soon, ABCL earned the tag of a 'sick' company with a debt of US$14m by the Indian Board for Industrial and Financial Reconstruction.

Bachchan's friends advised him to close ABCL venture and move on. But he decided to clear all its debts despite huge losses and re-start the production of films. Many businessmen and financial advisors joined in convincing AB to give up ABCL and start a new life. However, AB believed in *Repeat* and kept going. Forgetting the faith of the people in AB and ABCL was not easy for Bachchan. He felt that he owe people the money that they invested in him. He could not let it go easily. He felt a sword hanging on his head all the time, spending many sleepless nights. One of his old industry friends and a big film producer Yash Chopra offered him a role in his movie Mohabattein. Yash Chopra understood AB's situation of bankruptcy. At that time

Bachchan had no films, his house and a small property in New Delhi were attached.

After that Bachchan started doing commercials, television, and films with a big show Kaun Banega Crorepati (a franchise of Who's Wants to be a Millionaire) that's still going on after twenty years since 2000 launch. Today, Bachchan is happy as he has repaid his entire debt of Rs 90 crore and is a very successful artist with many endorsements, shows and films in his kitty.

Amitabh Bachchan, the star, refused to go down with the history as a failure even if ABCL was down and out. Kaun Banega Crorepati—a TV game show revived his fortunes along with those of the channel STAR Plus. In the year 2000, most big movie stars saw TV as a step back in their career. However, Bachchan turned that perception around. Rough estimates reveal that Bachchan is charging about Rs 5 crore per episode for the show. Endorsements like ICICI Bank worth Rs 10 crore, helped Big B pay back creditors and clean up ABCL's balance sheet. Today at the age of 76 and leaving Corona behind Amitabh Bachchan has emerged as a greater icon. He never shied away from taking the responsibility, demonstrating *Observe, Own* and *Fix* behaviours of *Working Clock* continuously.

In an interview in 2009, AB acknowledged "I think perhaps, in many ways, I should be the person bearing the blame I am not a businessman, I have never been. I have problems dealing with money. My entire career has been managed by family members or managers who have looked after my affairs. I am ignorant as far as money matters are concerned. For me to suddenly be thrown into this huge corporate ocean without adequate managerial capacity was perhaps the unmaking of the corporation. But I was told that 'You're like the brand figure, you don't have to get into the nitty-gritty of management. So, I very diligently kept away from it.

What was required was to have an efficient executive team where you have CEOs, VPs, etc., which is what I did. I entrusted them with the job of running the corporation. I am sorry to say, but despite all this talk of professional executives and professionalism in management, this was a terrible example as far as ABCL was concerned. I trusted them, but their feedback, their information was inadequate and false. It led to one disaster after another."

Amitabh Bachchan in 2001 relaunched ABCL as AB Corp. The company went on to produce hit films such as Paa in 2009.

He acknowledges that he got another chance to prove himself again. "Hum log chaas bhi phook phook kar piyenge abhi." (once bitten twice shy). He learned from his mistakes. He had gone through a bad phase, and he accepts his failure. He is keeping in his mind that he should not repeat past mistakes now. Today in 2020, rough estimates peg Bachchan family net worthat INR 3000 crores.

He Repeated the steps on *Working Clock*. Imagine if he would not have pulled himself back towards *Working Clock*, what consequences he, his family, and his brand value would have faced.

ACCOUNTABILITY RESILIENCE QUIZ

After reading AB's story, how about finding if you have it in you what AB demonstrated to pull back from *Stuck Clock* towards *Working Clock*. Let's do a small self-assessment to see how you score:

	Statements	Always	Mostly	At Times	Rarely	Never
1	You can sense the problems early on that can prevent you being pulled towards *Stuck Clock*	5	4	3	2	1
2	You have the ability and resilience to *Fix*, to avoid getting pulled on *Stuck Clock*	5	4	3	2	1
3	You diligently perform your responsibilities, irrespective of the results	5	4	3	2	1
4	You do not wait for instructions to perform your responsibilities	5	4	3	2	1
5	You help others around you in clarifying their responsibilities	5	4	3	2	1
6	You have the risk appetite to *Fix* it.	5	4	3	2	1
7	You do not give up on first hurdle, instead to pursue your endeavours to make it work	5	4	3	2	1
8	You not only have the ability but you keep checking your goals progress	5	4	3	2	1
9	In difficult situations, you remain result oriented to *Repeat*	5	4	3	2	1
10	You can consistently *Observe, Own, Fix and Repeat*	5	4	3	2	1

Once you complete the above assignment, total up your scores on each of the ten statements and refer the following scale to see your ability to stay on *Working Clock*:

Total Score	Interpretation
40-50	Denotes strong behaviours of *Observe, Own, Fix* and *Repeat.* You should remain focussed and not bother about the 'noise' around.
30-40	Denotes you have sufficient attitude to stay *Working Clock*, but you can improve
20-30	Indicates you face problem in taking risks for *Fixing.*
0-20	Indicates you could still be stuck on *Stuck Clock* behaviours. You need to go back and again read the chapters starting from *Observe*.

CIRCLING BACK TO MAHABHARATA

How to go about your life, Mahabharata presents us with a nearly perfect example except, of course, the war. The war of Kurukshetra, which was one of the bloodiest ever fought in human history. Myth has that it wiped out 80 per cent of the entire Indian male population, while it lasted only eighteen days. The war story forms more than a quarter of the epic. Most people know that after the war, the Pandavas won and the Kauravas lost. Let's us find some answers to know How long did the Pandavas rule Hastinapur? What happened to Pandavas after their win? Who all survived? What happened with Lord Krishna? Well, here are the (probable) answers.

1. Pandavas were crowned the rulers of Hastinapur after winning the war of Kurukshetra.

2. Yudhishthira was crowned as king, but a grief-stricken Gandhari curses Krishna wishing for him and the whole Yadav clan a painful death just like her sons, Kauravas.

3. Pandavas went on to rule Hastinapur for 36 years. In the meantime, Gandhari's curse to Lord Krishna starts taking shape. Krishna after witnessing ominous events in Dwarka, lead the entire Yadav clan to Prabhasa. In Prabhasa, a murderous rebellion started amongst the clan. The Yadavs ended up killing each other to the extent of almost wiping out their entire race.

4. While trying to extinguish the rebellion, a hunter mistakenly shoots an arrow at the 'mortal' Lord Krishna, ultimately killing him. Thereafter, Krishna merges in the image of Vishnu and leaves his mortal human body. After the demise of Lord Krishna, Ved Vyasa tells Arjun that the purpose of his and his brothers' lives is over.

When we can move towards *Working Clock* following all four steps, *Observe, Own, Fix* and *Repeat,* we do not need a 'Krishna' to guide us every time. Organisations and people who have not only understood but implemented the steps over and over again makes it a process. They do not fail to *Observe* the first signs of trouble. After *Observing,* they very well know that they have to *Own* the circumstances, what is expected from them. Once Owned, they also have the experience of *Fix*ing it with the right attitude and behaviours. After *Fix*ing, they do not rest; instead, they *Repeat* to ensure that the changes are well-entrenched and become part of the routine. Before proceeding to the last and final chapter of the book, let us read a story of a team that imbibed *Repeat* in themselves. *Repeat* is part of the group culture in whatever they do.

CASE STUDY : CHEF HEMANT OBEROI STORY

When the bullets started firing just after 9 pm on November 26 2008, Hemant Oberoi stayed calm. For hours, as terrorists took hostages and killed indiscriminately across Mumbai, the chef and other staff at the Taj Mahal Palace Hotel did everything they could to keep others safe. Despite being in a position to leave, Chef Oberoi chose to stay. "What else can you do?" he says. "We had to protect our guests." He followed *"Atithi Devo Bhava"* Atithi Devo Bhava, also spelt Atithidevo Bhava, English transliteration: You become the one who considers that Guests are equivalent to God), prescribes a dynamic of the host-guest relationship which embodies the traditional Indian Hindu-Buddhist philosophy of revering guests with the same respect as a God. This concept of going out of the way to treat guests with reverence goes even beyond the traditional Hindu-Buddhist common greeting of Namaste (I bow to the divinity in you) used for everyone.

The attack on the Taj was one of a series of coordinated shootings and bombings; a group of terrorists from Pakistan targeting locations including a restaurant, a hospital, a busy train station, a Jewish community centre, and taxis, as well as the landmark luxury hotel.

It was the start of what would become a three-day siege, the local police ill-equipped to deal with an attack on such a large scale. At least 166 people were killed across the city, with hundreds more wounded. The opulent Taj hotel was full of people from all over the world when the terrorists arrived there. As well as those staying and working at the venue, people from outside had run to the building as bullets rained down, believing it would be the best place to stay safe. Gunmen seized the hotel with hundreds of people trapped inside, firing and hurling grenades at random.

Thirty-two people there were among those killed, but hundreds more were saved. It's a story of how Chef Oberoi and many of his staff risked their lives to protect their guests.

"I stayed, and it was the right thing to do. It wasn't a question of bravery" Chef Oberoi had heard gunshots before, knew the sound of bombs exploding. Growing up in India in Punjab, he was all too aware of the sounds of conflict. So when the acclaimed chef realised what was happening inside the Taj on the night of the attacks, he did not panic. Chef Oberoi was a renowned chef in India who had served everyone from Angelina Jolie, and Brad Pitt to Barack Obama and Princess Diana is very much real.

Recalling the events of the night, Chef Oberoi says: "When I heard the gunshots, I said, 'Close the doors. Make sure the lights are switched off'. That was my first reaction. We tried to secure areas as much as we could. In my childhood, I have seen all sorts of things. I have heard gunshots before; I know the sound of gunshots and bombs falling. There was also the '93 attack in Mumbai. But this was different because we had so many guests and their lives were in danger. Anyone who walks into your house is your guest, and that's how it was. You have to protect them. That was my worry. It would have been very easy for me to leave. I was 20 seconds away from the exit door. It would have been easy, but if I had left, everyone [all the staff] would have left too. Most of the time, I was very, very calm; that is just what I am like. I don't think I have raised my voice many times in my life. My philosophy is that if you don't understand my silence, then you won't understand my words. If I had panicked or reacted differently, the whole team would have been affected. It was my responsibility. Even in the morning, at about 4 am, when the terrorists came into the kitchen area, and they were shooting people.

All I wanted was to make sure people were okay. I had my family at home, but I still say my priority was the guests. I never thought about anything else, and I couldn't. I had to make sure people were safe. I think it was the right thing to do. It wasn't a question of bravery. I was responsible for people. All I did is what I think people should do; it wasn't brave. They killed seven of my chefs, some of the guests. I salute my colleagues who laid down their lives to help. I'm very proud of the team I had. Through thick and thin, they were with me. I had one colleague who wasn't well; he was having dialysis once a week. I told him to go, but he stayed. We had a team spirit."

Eventually, as the sun was coming up after almost 12 hours, the chef and his staff were able to lead the last of the people he had been protecting in an escape down a stairwell. When he felt he was able to leave the hotel himself, he rushed home, he says. It was the first time he had ever done so without changing out of his uniform. "I lived only a few minutes away, and there were about 25 or 30 people at my home when I got there. I hadn't been able to speak to my wife so when I got there, and they thought they had seen a ghost. She was very relieved to know I was safe. It was very frightening for her. You're not bothered about yourself. But when they were running, firing, you think maybe we won't survive. You don't know. It all happens very quickly."

Chef Oberoi was determined to help rebuild the hotel after the attack and worked to get the first restaurant open again just three weeks later. "We were so angry, when we went back, seeing the bloodshed," he says. "It was riddled with bullets. I said we have to get back; we cannot let this get us down, we get back as if nothing has happened. We will never be scared. In 21 days, we were back. We laid down in a circle, thinking this is it. We are going to die".

And the attackers, these were young boys, being ordered to kill people. They were fighting among themselves; some of them didn't want to kill people. They were victims too. It's not them to be blamed; it's the people behind it. It's the people who were pushing them.

The only gunman to survive, Mohammed Ajmal Kasab, was hanged in 2012 for several offences including waging war against India, murder, and terrorist acts.

Isn't it mesmerising about this idea where you had all these people from all these different walks of life, who you would expect in these kinds of situations - where the bullets are flying, the bombs are dropping - that everyone would be in it for themselves. But something very counter-intuitive happened, where you had regular, everyday people, selflessly protecting one another and being there for one another—both guests and staff. Chef Oberoi was a living example of *Accountability* and ownership at the display. He was well trained in all four steps of *Working Clock* behaviours.

When he *Observed* the situation, he knew that he has to *Own*. He not only Owned for himself but also made his team *Own* up. After he and his team Owned up the situation, they knew it's time to *Fix* the situation by ensuring that minimum guests get impacted by the attack. Once *Fix*ed, they went on to *Repeat* by ensuring that the iconic restaurant in the hotel comes up back to its glory in three weeks. Such people not only follow the behaviours of *Working Clock* but also live them every day. Chef Oberoi did not get any lesson in the form of Gita from Krishna, since he was part of the culture of the group and the society that follow Atithi Devo Bhava.

PART

III

Putting it all together

CHAPTER

8

PREPARING EVERYONE IN THE ORGANISATION AND IN SOCIETY FOR MOVING LIKE A WORKING CLOCK

PREPARING EVERYONE IN THE ORGANISATION AND IN SOCIETY FOR MOVING LIKE A WORKING CLOCK

L ike 'Lord' Krishna helped Arjun to *Observe, Own, Fix,* and *Repeat.* He made Arjun's journey toward the realization that he already possessed the power to get the results he sought, never intervening unless necessary. Krishna didn't tell him everything at the beginning because he knew how important it was for them to develop their Arjun's sense of powerfulness, but neither did he refuse to help when he saw that the Arjun had reached a point where he could apply the resources he could bring to bear. By so doing, he symbolizes the leader who operates from Working Clock.

MOVING PEOPLE FROM VICTIM TO ACCOUNTABILITY MINDSET

So far, in this book, we discussed how you could get towards *Working Clock.* Now, as Krishna, how every leader in the company can help others to discover the benefits of working with behaviours on *Working Clock.* How can you, as a leader, make people get out of the victim and circumstances behaviours to achieve what they would enjoy? Leaders operating on *Working Clock* display some consistent behaviours, even if at times they fail, but never stay at failure for long. They never speak the victim language; they help others to move and stay on *Working Clock.* They constantly seek and provide feedback both for engagement and setting the compass right. They hold themselves as accountable as everyone else. Let's understand how the victim attitude can make even the fiercest of animals lose to dogs in this short story:

LIFE THREATENING *ACCOUNTABILITY*

Owing Covid19 lockdown across the country for months, the state government banned any circus shows. The circus team was a huge team of about seventy people and about the same number of animals and birds. Now, like humans, they felt that they can still do something else for a living, but the animals would die if they do not get proper food. The circus owners decided to release all animals, about nine lions, twelve elephants, various horses, and birds into the jungle. Days passed, and one of the erstwhile circus employees heard a terrible story. He was informed by the village near the jungle that those lions were killed and eaten by the wild dogs. As lions, while remaining in the cage most of the time, were fed meat and they never had to hunt. On the other side, the wild dogs were always hunting in the jungle. They did not even spare the lions since there was no resistance or fight from the lions.

ACCOUNTABILITY – NOT A CHOICE ANYMORE

Building *Accountability* is not a choice anymore. In a recently concluded annual general meeting with the top management of Tata Motors shareholders questioned the top management about their dividends. The company has not been able to register handsome profits for a few years, some of it attributed to the Jaguar acquisition and thus paying any sizeable dividend. The shareholders questioned the top management on their annual package and why it should not be reduced. The principle is clear if you don't deliver your responsibility, you will be held accountable, and you will have to face the consequences.

Thus, from the last three to four decades, companies have started passing on the P&L responsibility to virtually every employee in the company. If every employee in the company is not aligned with the business objective, and leaders do not prepare everyone in their teams. *Accountability* questions by shareholders would continue to be raised. This increasing emphasis on responsive leadership at the top has been further fuelled by the power shift taking place in most organizations in which senior executives are spreading decision-making authority more widely to the lowest levels of the enterprise. This naturally is making, *Working Clock* leadership as a requirement.

One of the elements we will discuss in this chapter is if accountable leadership is a choice or not. If any leader has learned the steps to shift towards *Working Clock*, isn't it natural for them to transfer this knowledge to their teams? Otherwise, what's the use of a few people moving to *Working Clock* and others suffer from *Stuck Clock* behaviours.

The first step a *Working Clock* leader would have learned is to *Observe*, which means that now that leader is equipped to *Observe* the *Stuck Clock* behaviours. Thus, you know when to intervene on victim stories. However, for that first, you have to get out of your comfort zone like Sanjeev Bikhchandani displayed earlier in the book. You have to go and find out what is keeping people saddled in victim stories. You have to rip apart the stories and find the real problems and make them address those problems. While at a 'lower' level, they have to rise above the smoke screens, go wider to see the real problem. They have to rise above the haze to see where the problem is.

These *Working Clock* leaders do not buy the stories that it has always been done like this; this is the best we can do; we do not have the required resources to produce quality stuff. They can sense victim behaviours, and they know that they have to start coaching them to move towards *Working Clock*. While doing so, they do not go overboard. Practised intervention requires a delicate yet firm touch.

Some people may hide behind their personal or physical inability situations to shelter under the victim umbrella. A leader having learned the *Working Clock* behaviours know very well that only that situation is not responsible for the current situation. They also know how to keep that difficult situation aside and motivate people to still move towards *Working Clock* behaviours.

While trying to move people towards *Working Clock*, make sure that you do not press the panic button. Remember it's a behaviour change, and it takes time. You can't make people more effective, more knowledgeable, more righteous, braver, more productive, friendlier, more trustworthy, or in any other way more "correct." The right way is to coach, train, give feedback, and encourage them. *Working Clock* leaders also recognize that everything is not in their control. Like the ongoing pandemic, nobody would have prepared to handle it. Other things like weather, accidents, wars, are not in one's control. Intelligent leaders do not fret over the parameters that are not in their control. These leaders sharp focus on those that are directly under their control. Many people are not able to accept the reality that both controllable and uncontrollable factors confront everyone. It's the ability to separate the two help one to shift to *Working Clock* behaviours.

COACHING PEOPLE FOR WORKING CLOCK BEHAVIOURS

Stephen Covey says that all things are created twice: first, the mental conceptualization and visualization and a second physical, actual creation. Becoming your creator means to plan and visualize what you're going to do and what you're setting out to accomplish and then go out and creating it. Effective leaders understand the delicate but firm touch they need to shift people towards *Working Clock*. They know that before they start coaching others, they consider this list:

9X *ACCOUNTABILITY* COACHING LIST

1. People are ready to take honest and constructive feedback for moving towards *Working Clock*They do not wait for providing feedback on the progress made, they do the same with their supervisors as well
2. They are open to receive feedback from others if they are on *Working Clock*
3. They constantly ask themselves how they can do better
4. They never shy in accepting the mistake with the purpose of growth
5. They focus on outcomes and issues instead of people
6. They acknowledge that people may be in different personal situations and use the discretion accordingly
7. Like a mother knows when to stir in the pan and when to reduce the flame, they know the usage of flame for the right amount of time and intensity
8. They know that one size doesn't fit all for coaching
9. They accept the diversity in capabilities of their people

Above are the basics for any leader to embark on the coaching journey.

Like coaching, the shift to *Working Clock* requires patience, nurturing, and follow-up. While coaching people, you are making them independent of you and not dependent upon you. While you are available during the learning phase, but you also have a clear 'exit' date for making them accountable. As a coach, you appreciate that the people could be fighting to detach from years of behaviours and may take some time. During coaching, they know that there's a problem, and both of you are trying to find the best solution for the big picture. You are moving them from micro to macro view of their contribution.

There could be a situation that one of your people and you would have worked together at the same level in the past. In case you have shared the victim stories in the past, the coaching would not be easy. Other people would always look at you with suspicion. In such situations, we always recommend someone else in the organization or an external coach to do the coaching for the best results. However, if you do not see any such issues, make sure that you follow the below framework diligently:

COACHING FRAMEWORK

1. **Ask** – Instead of making any assumptions, hearsay, best is to ask the person yourself. While doing so, make sure that you are moving the individual towards a positive and abundant options scenario.

2. **Listen** – Initially, you have to sympathetically listen to their victim story, give them space to elaborate within a timeframe. Understand why they feel stuck like a *Stuck Clock*.

3. **Acknowledge** – Do not belittle their situation or take it lightly. Instead, share your own experience if you had been in their situation and how you came out of it. Accept that their challenges are real and both of you are committed to finding a solution for it.

4. **Coach** – Once you have created a safe, trustworthy, and positive environment only then start coaching. Help them understand how you followed the four steps of *Observe, Own, Fix,* and *Repeat* to move towards *Working Clock*. Link the significance of each step in progress towards the *Working Clock* and the benefits attached. You may have to spend some time to explain the concept of *Stuck Clock* and *Working Clock*, make that investment.

5. **Commit** – Ensure that both of you are committed to the benefits of operating on *Working Clock*, how it can be a life-changing experience.

WORKING ON CULTURE CHANGE AT AN ORGANIZATION

Most organizations have a vision, the reason they exist. This vision helps to give a proper structure to the organization. It's like starting a family having a vision. Some families live with happiness and prosperity while others keep fighting, even if they live together.

Company culture is a combination of vision, values, work environment, and behaviours at play. It is the identity of your company. It is known for:

- How people feel about your company.
- How it functions.
- How it connects with its customers.
- What makes it stand out?
- What's the perception of your company for various stakeholders?
- What's your company's reputation?

COMPANY CULTURE AND ITS IMPORTANCE

One company can have great resources and talent; it may still fail if it lacks a strong company culture. Companies like Apple, Google, Amazon, or Disney, are having a common thread that makes them great; it's their culture. Starting with a vision, these companies, over the years, build a strong company culture. They know the value of their brands, what it stands for. They know the message they want to spread to its customers. Their employees are provided with perhaps the best benefits and perks to take care of. Respect for employees' decisions is a promoted culture. They appreciate the importance of working collaboratively with respect and trust.

Once, Apple's ex CEO, Steve Jobs, said that Apple has a very collaborative company culture and does not have any committees. People at Apple work like a start-up, where people work individually for their different products and services for their part. Enough trust and belief make them do so well in making Apple one of the most prominent Fortune 500 Company.

Apple, the #4 Fortune 500 in 2020, has been following this organizational culture since its inception. It proves that Apple was not only sure about its company culture but also how it would want to function. Like Steve Jobs said, they believe in collaborative teamwork, and all its employees are aligned in the company's vision. The products they churn out, they trust and are proud of it, which reflects in it. This sense of vision and culture made Apple, the no.1 technology company in the world.

SIX WAYS TO BUILD A STRONG COMPANY CULTURE

1. **Build a strong foundation** – As a building rests on its foundation, your company rests on the foundational beliefs you have. You can structure it the way you want like a building design. The vision can come from the 'looks' that an individual or group may follow. The foundation should have these core principles. This sets the base of the culture you would like to follow and work towards it.

2. **Choose right people** – Every company represents the traits of its employees and their understanding of corporate culture and behaviour. Therefore, it is important to persistently create a culture that goes with the company's vision and values. This would help your organization stand tall amongst its peers. Employing the right people who fit with your organization's philosophies is a great tactic to follow. A wrong hire can completely spoil the culture for you, hire people who fit your culture. Someone who believes in your vision and work towards it

3. **Company Vision** – Company vision statement describes where the company wants a community, or the world, to be as a result of the company's services. Having the right vision is the key when you want to start a strong company culture. The vision statements usually carry a broad purpose.

4. **Your brand Cause** – You have to explain to people the cause your brand stands for. How your brand addresses or solves people's problems? Or how does it serve the customer? These type of questions, while may sound very moralistic but it is very important for any organization. It connects people with the brand as to what it stands for. For example, the Tata brand reminds people of trust. Maruti-Suzuki reminds people of value for money, while Benz represents luxury.

5. **Engaged employees** – Multiple examples in corporations would tell us that the companies where employees are productively engaged, they tend to perform better. An engaged employee is not only working for a salary but also for the purpose. Make sure that you are engaging employees beyond work requirements. Caring for employees would reward you with much bigger results compared to the costs incurred.

6. **Retaining talent** – A CFO asked a CEO what if we train people and they leave, the CEO replied, what if we do not train and they stay. This statement sums up the message towards the value of the talent. During the ongoing pandemic, governments could build makeshift hospitals, ventilators, PPE kits (Personal Protection Equipment), and many other physical infrastructures. But a very senior doctor asked, how will you 'produce' doctors and nurses who are required to run that infrastructure.

Only when you have a strong company culture, you can expect people to shift to *Working Clock*. Culture building takes a long time. Organizational culture sets the roadmap for everything an enterprise does. Industries and situations may vary significantly; there is no one-size-fits-all culture template that meets the needs of all organizations. A strong culture is a common factor among the most successful companies. Everybody at the top has consensus regarding cultural priorities, and those values focus not on employees but the organization and its goals.

As they say, the character of a person is only tested in difficult times. Similarly, the ongoing pandemic of Covid-19 is presenting an unprecedented situation in front of companies. This is the time their real culture would be observed. Strong companies with a strong culture have not fired people in haste. They have managed the situation by open communication, taking drastic steps, cutting discretionary expenses, etc. instead of going in for layoffs. All four steps on *Working Clock*, *Observe*, *Own*, *Fix*, and *Repeat* come to play when a culture is tested.

How to embark on a journey of *Fix*ing the progressive culture can be separately planned and executed with the authors. While *Accountability* is one of the strong pillars of culture building, it requires much more than only building *Accountability*.

APPLYING WORKING CLOCK STEPS TO CORPORATE INDIA ISSUES

Greta Thunberg, possibly the youngest environment warrior and forest fires in the jungles of have resulted in the environment drawing the attention of company boards as well as the investing world. In contrast, concerns related to governance continue to rule the roost in India. It remains the single-most-important challenge for Indian companies because of its adverse impact on the bourses. Ten per cent of companies of the Nifty-50 index is facing corporate governance issues and have faced value erosion on the bourses. Issues related to climate change, pollution, and employment are yet to become a worry for India Inc. and its investors – even though as a country India is facing challenges related to pollution, erratic monsoon, and unemployment.

Khaitan & Co is amongst India's oldest and full-service law firms comprising over 530 fee earners and consultants including 115 partners and directors. Established over a hundred years ago in 1911 by Debi Prasad Khaitan. Mr Kahitan was a member of the Constituent Assembly of India and one of the seven members of the Drafting Committee which framed the Constitution of India. Based out of Mumbai, it's partner Kalpana Unadkat with Pranay Bagdi, Senior Associate, listed down the top 8 issues faced in India on *Accountability* and Corporate governance.

TOP 8 *ACCOUNTABILITY* ISSUES FACING CORPORATE INDIA

1. Beginning from the top

Company board of directors and their role is the foundation for good corporate governance. Law has been enacted in the Companies Act to have a good mix of executive and non-executive directors. It also stipulates the requirement of at least one woman director on the board for diversity. We all know the importance of a capable, diverse, and active board would, to a large extent, improve the stewardship standards of the company. However, improving compliance "in spirit" remains a challenge towards implanting governance in companies' cultures. Compliance requirement of diversity in the board of directors for most companies remains on paper.

Appointments to the board are still carried out by fellow board member recommendations or by way of "word of mouth". Friends and family of 'promoters' (a uniquely Indian term for controlling shareholders including founders) occupying the board member seats are quite common in family-run companies. It's time that the boards are also subjected to performance evaluation as a minimum benchmark for director appointment. Another solution for instance, - rating board diversity and governance practices and publishing such results could be the innovation. This is the stage to *Observe* for planning to shift towards *Working Clock*.

2. Directors Performance Evaluation

While performance evaluation of directors has been part of the existing legal framework in India, it caught the regulator's attention three years ago. A 'Guidance Note on Board Evaluation' was released in January 2017 by SEBI, India's capital markets regulator. Various aspects of performance evaluation by laying down the means to identify objectives, different criteria, and methods of evaluation were elaborated in this note. There has been a constant expectation from pubic to know how the performance evaluation to achieve the desired results on governance practices, has been achieved.

Like in performance evaluation of executives, the board's evaluation continues to be a sensitive subject. Especially it's public disclosure may become counterproductive. Directors peer review having negative feedback, to avoid public scrutiny, may not be shared. To negate this behaviour, the role of independent directors in performance evaluation is key. Its time-independent directors *Own* this up and ensure that the performance is not only evaluated for compliance but in spirit. Failing to do this, will continue to have corporate debacles, as discussed in earlier chapters.

3. Independent Directors - Really?

Eighteen years ago, independent directors' appointment was supposed to be the biggest corporate governance reform. However, independent directors have hardly been able to make the expected impact, even after eighteen long years. Regulators like SEBI have been, time and again, made the norms tighter. They introduced a comprehensive definition of independent directors. Audit committee's role was crystalized apart from other changes. However, for most Indian promoter companies, the compliance has remained a tick-the-box approach towards the regulatory requirements. It is very unlikely that the independent directors, appointed by the promoters, will stand-up and raise the flag for minority interests against the promoters. While the regulator has brought various reforms in compliance, its role still leaves a vacuum. Perhaps, limiting the promoter's powers in matters relating to independent directors and their appointment can be explored. This means that if the problem is not *Observed* and *Owned*, it cannot be *Fix*ed to move towards *Working Clock*.

4. Removal of Independent Directors

Removal of independent directors by promoters is common in a situation where they tend to disagree with the promoters. At the same time, independent directors have been frequently questioned for not playing an active role on the board. Current law provisions allow the removal of the independent director or majority shareholders easily.

This fundamental conflict has a direct impact on the independence of directors and hence leaving a hurdle to *Fix* it. To increase in transparency about appointment and removal of directors, even SEBI's International Advisory Board proposed it in 2017. Safeguarding independent directors from disputation action and allow them greater freedom of action, it is important to have additional checks in the process of their removal - for instance, requiring approval of the majority of public shareholders.

5. *Accountability* to Stakeholders

Independent directors cannot look the other way from *Accountability* towards the shareholders and the public in general. They need to be empowered with greater responsibilities and duties. Continuing in the same spirit, Indian company law updated in 2013 stipulated that directors are dutybound not only towards the shareholders and company management but also towards the community, and protection of the environment. While these duties are applicable for all directors, but directors remained complacent in the absence of enforcement action. If all general meetings are represented by the full board, stakeholders can interact and question the board about their *Accountability* towards mentioned responsibilities.

6. Executive Remuneration

Executive remuneration has remained a contentious issue, especially towards stakeholders *Accountability*. At the same time, it is true that companies have to offer competitive compensation for attracting the best talent. However, stakeholders would always like to see it linked to business success. Under the present Indian laws, the remuneration of key employees is decided by the nomination and remuneration committee (a committee formed by the board comprising of a majority of independent directors).

This remuneration is also required to be made public. However, this mandate may not be sufficient for transparency and win the trust of the stakeholders. Perhaps, linking the remuneration with the stakeholders' approval can fill the present trust deficit. Like we discussed in the previous chapter, how a very reputed one of the largest automobile companies faced tough questions on executive compensation during the Annual General Meeting. This shows that if companies fail to *Observe* and *Fix*, shareholders will remind them.

7. Founders' Control and Succession Planning

In India, the founders' ability to control the affairs of the company has the potential of derailing the entire corporate governance system. Unlike developed economies, the identity of the founder and the company is often merged in India. Founders or promoters, irrespective of their legal position, have a habit of exercising their significant influence towards the majority of the business decisions of companies. They fail to accept the need for succession planning. If founders create a succession plan and implement it, it will be a game-changer from the governance and business continuity perspective. Family-owned Indian companies suffer an inherent inhibition to let go of control. One of the ways to address could be to widen the shareholder base - as PE and other institutional investors pump in the capital, founders are forced to think about a succession plan and step away with dignity. Until founders see the benefits of the required behaviours for the *Working Clock* approach, the problems appear to remain.

8. Risk Management

With the Indian media's tremendous growth over the years, it has lead to large businesses exposed to real-time monitoring by both business and national media. Devising and implementing a risk management policy is necessary for the given scenario since the board is only playing an oversight role in the affairs of a company. A statement from the board, in its report to the shareholders indicating the development and implementation of risk management policy for the company, is required in this context, as per Indian company law. For assessing the risk management systems of the company, the independent directors are mandated to do so. A strong risk management policy that spells out key guiding principles and practices for mitigating risks in day-to-day activities is imperative for a governance model to be effective. While this is a great policy, it can be followed simply by following the steps of the *Working Clock* approach, *Observe, Own, Fix,* and *Repeat.*

CONCLUSION

India, over the years, has witnessed many enactments like the modified Companies Act, 2013. SEBI's listing obligations and disclosure requirements regulations. These enactments have contributed significantly to strengthening governance norms and in increasing *Accountability* by way of disclosures towards structural and regulatory changes. These changes are based on the Anglo-Saxon model of corporate governance. This could probably be one of the key reasons behind current practices of corporate governance, not achieving the desired level of fulfilment. This should be coupled with the board and the promoters' embracing such reforms - in form and spirit of *Working Clock* behaviours for achieving desired results. Regulatory measures must be modelled based on the practices and business environment in India. Remember, only when you assume full *Accountability* for your feelings, thoughts, actions, and results can you direct your destiny; otherwise, someone or something else will.

Accountability at a corporate level is expected and governed by different corporate laws statutory agencies. What about the people in general. Are we anywhere closer to the Japanese culture where people take social *Accountability* the same as they do at their homes? Let's look at the pandemic situation in early September of 2020. India is number two in the maximum cases around the world with 42 million total cases, only behind the USA with 64.5 million. Compare this with Japan's impacted cases 0.07 million cases. So, the positivity percentage to the population in Japan is 0.057% while in India it is 0.306%. Yes, India is the second-most populous country after China in the world, the majority of the population lives in rural areas, but that that cannot be an excuse for such a high impact rate. What is it then?

To expect Indians to show total conformity to the preventive measures against COVID 19, announced by the Indian government is like expecting a little too much. Basic safety measures such as wearing a mask in public spaces, social distancing, self-isolation, or quarantining (in either symptomatic or asymptomatic cases) and getting tested if showing symptoms are some of the important guidelines All of us Indians are expected to wash our hands frequently with soap; sanitize our living and workspaces, including the surfaces we frequently touch during our activities.

While some people follow these guidelines meticulously, a majority of Indians flout them frequently. Social distancing is not always observed when people are generally present in public spaces or parks. People do not wear mask often because people say it's difficult to breathe or unhealthy.

They feel it doesn't make much of a difference—other more disturbing violations such as people running from hospitals while in quarantine. People were becoming violent when questioned why they were not following the guidelines. Initially, when the pandemic began, people made a deliberate attempt to hide their symptoms or their contact history. Cases of mass gathering, parties, and get-togethers were also reported.

This brings us to a significant question: How are people expected to be Accountable in difficult times? Aren't we, as a society, expected to behave responsibly? Even when things are normal, Indians take special pride in flouting norms or the rules, without bothering about our society and adopting an 'I, me, and myself' approach. Jumping the queue or the traffic signal not worrying about accidents or inconvenience caused to others. Indians take most things as "chalta hai". We follow the law to avoid punishment and not in spirit, a fact demonstrated by the Indian police using batons to force the people to stay indoors during the lockdowns. It was only the fear of the stick and not a concern for others that kept people from stepping out of their homes. Governments in different states had to threaten people with monetary and disciplinary actions to make them stay indoors.

When the Prime Minister requested people show some respect for corona warrior by beating thalis or lighting candles, they hit the roads in large groups to celebrate, throwing all social distancing rules out of the window. They started gathering in groups in their respective residential societies, apartments or streets as if the crisis got over, and it was time for celebration and victory. This, in turn, defeated the very purpose for which our Prime Minister had given the call. It is quite evident that the society which doesn't follow the rules and has scant regard for the principle of collective social *Accountability* and responsibility in the normal times is surely bound to falter in times of a crisis as severe as the Covid-19 pandemic. Unfortunately, such behaviours were observed across the world, even in the most developed countries.

In such critical times, what is important to understand is that our actions have negative outcomes. These outcomes are not harmful only for us but also for others. A single mistake in terms of socially unaccountable behaviour would not only cost us dear, but also take a heavy toll on our citizens, our neighbours, and our community. This kind of lack of social *Accountability* has been demonstrated by all sections of our society, illiterate, semi-literate, educated, and highly skilled professionals. This is a moment of thinking for all of us, and we must ponder upon how can we not only help ourselves but also those around us.

Fear of law cannot become the reigning principle of regulating human behaviour in a society. Eventually, all civilized societies depend upon the consciousness of the individual citizens and also on their ability to organize themselves in a free, fair, and yet accountable manner. Fear cannot be used as a warning to prevent dangerous and aggressive behaviour in the face of the Covid-19 pandemic. It is time that the citizens should understand their role and *Accountability* in controlling the spread and transmission of Covid-19.

The government cannot be present to correct its citizens in all situations; eventually, all the citizens must come forward to fulfil our social responsibility and *Accountability*. All it requires is some deep reflection and cultivation of restraint, taking the law in spirit, and the ability to feel for and connect with our fellow citizens. This is too serious about being left to the prudence or fancies of the individuals. To achieve this social objective, the Indian government has come up with a new education policy that's a shift away from rote learning. Its focus is more on vocational and behavioural skills; it will hopefully address some of these issues for the generations to come. We can incorporate the community benefit practices into our education system, right from the primary stage. This will should help our future citizens develop a strong sense of ethics and be more accountable.

We chose epic Mahabharata to drive the lessons on *Accountability* for people to see the cost of not being Accountable. Whether its king Dhritrashtra, Bhishmpitamha, Guru Dronacharya, Yudhishthir, Duryodhan, or prince Arjun, whoever has compromised the *Accountability*, it lead to the bloodiest war on the face of mankind. Every generation is not going to get Krishna to come and give Gita sermons, awaken Arjun to stand up, and fulfil their *Accountability*. Like we have studied various examples in the book, the menace of being unaccountable is spread across individuals, geographies, companies, families, societies, and countries. It's time we all collectively stand up and move towards *Working Clock* behaviours to become accountable.

As we write the end piece, we only know that it's just the beginning. Like we learned in the book that to be fully effective and to progress like a Working Clock, we need to embrace all four steps of Accountability in all our actions and thoughts.

Background Note for Readers

Our book uses extensive references from Mahabharata. This note will help you make sense of the references that you might read in the book. The epic Mahabharta the longest epic available in history, has about 200 characters. We are discussing the story and characters only relevant for our book purpose in this note.

ABOUT *DHARMA & KARMA*

Before understanding the epic *Mahabharata* and its main characters, let us understand the underlying philosophy of this epic. Like the other epic *Ramayana*, that's based upon the rights and wrongs, *Mahabharata* is based upon *Dharma* and *Karma*. The epic underlines the importance of one's Karma or expected *Accountability* in all situations. Apart from the main and most popular section *Bhagwat Gita*, there are many sub-sections underlying the importance of standing up to fulfil one's *Accountability* in all situations. Krishna assures Arjuna that this particular battle is righteous and he must fight as his duty or *Dharma* as a warrior. Arjun's *Dharma* was to fight in the battle because he was a warrior, but he must fight with detachment from the results of his actions and within the rules of the warriors' *Dharma*. *Bhagwat Gita*, as one of the main sections, underlines the relation between *Dharma* and *Karma*. Lord Krishna explains this in the beginning to Arjun with this shloka:

Karmanye vadhika raste, Ma phaleshu kadachana
Ma karma phala he tur bhuh, ma te sangotsva karmanye

Addressing the Arjun's dilemma, before the battle begins, Lord Krishna explains to Arjun the theory of *Karma*. Lord Krishna explains to Arjun to believe in himself and do your *Karma* (action).

Success will follow you eventually. Doing our *Karma* is in our hands only, Result is not in our hands.

THE MAHABHARATA

The Mahabharata is one of the oldest and the most popular mythology story of India along with The *Ramayana*. It was written by rishi (sage) Vyasa around the thirds century BC in Sanskrit. This story addresses the *Itihaas* (history) and *Dharma* (morality or righteousness). However, owing to its age, some question if the entire epic was written by Vyasa or there were many others who contributed to it.

Pandavas and Kauravas are two groups of cousins struggling for political power, the right and wrong makes the foundation of this Mahabharata epic. It is the longest epic in the world history that has about 1, 00,000 Sanskrit language couplets divided into eighteen sections.

THE BACKSTORY OF THE MAHABHARATA

As per Hindu cosmology that has four yugas or eras this story belongs to *Dvapar Yuga* (second era), Shanthanu was the ruling king of the Bharatvarsha (the Indian subcontinent as we see it today). Shanthanu's popularity was the subject of envy even amongst the Gods. Shanthanu married Goddess Ganga (the human form of the holy river Ganges). However, there was a binding condition to their marriage that the king would allow Ganga to do whatever she feels like without questioning. Any time if he questions or objects, she would leave him forever.

THE BIRTH OF BHISHMA

Shanthanu and Ganga were blessed with a child making the king very happy. But Ganga had some other plans; she threw the baby into the Ganges River. Bound by the marriage condition, Shanthanu could not ask her the reason. The eighth time Shanthanu could not control himself and objected when Ganga again tried to throw the newborn into the river. This break of marriage condition made Ganga leave Shanthanu with the newborn within Ganga river. A few years later, she returned the child to the king. Shanthanu named this child as Ganga Datta or gift of Ganga.

Years later Shanthanu met Sathiavathy, another very beautiful woman, a daughter of a fisherman. Shanthanu wished to marry her. However, her father laid down the condition to make her children the heirs of Shanthanu's kingdom. Ganga Datta was the eldest son and the legitimate heir to the kingdom and the successor to the throne. When Ganga Datta came to know the dilemma his father is facing, he took an oath to never marry or be a king; however, would always protect the kingdom. This hard oath made him Bhishma, as he was referred later on after taking the oath.

THE BIRTH OF DHRITRASHTRA AND PANDU

Sathyavathy delivered two children, and one of them died early. The other child was born with a very delicate mind and body. It was very difficult to find any girl for him to marry. Bhishma had to bring three young women to him by force; Amba, Ambika, and Ambalika to have a legitimate heir to the kingdom. However, Amba was allowed to go back to her lover, while the other two had to marry Vichitra Veerya. Owing to his condition, he was not able to produce any children. Hence, sage Vyasa was called in to bless the girls to conceive. However, when Ambika saw the sage, she closed her eyes, so she births to a blind child Dhritarashtra. Ambalika turned pale on seeing the sage that led her to give birth to pale coloured, Pandu.

THE RIVALRY BEGINS

Dhritrashtra and **Pandu** went to marry Gandhari and Kunthi, respectively. Gandhari gave birth to one hundred sons and a daughter, while Kunthi had five sons by the blessing of the Gods. This sets the ground for the epic *Mahabharata*. The sons of Dhritarashtra were called **Kauravas** while **Pandavas** were named after their father, Pandu. Pandavas, the sons of Dhritarashtra were more than equal to the Kauravas. The struggle for supremacy with *Dharma* and *Karma* between these two groups of cousins is the central theme of the *Mahabharata*.

LORD KRISHNA

Krishna's role in the Mahabharata gives direction to chaos while being at the centre of it. In Mahabharata, God is making shown bad decisions, directing a human to slaughter his kin all in the name of Dharma. There is a dichotomy to this: in one story, after the war Arjun breaks down with lament asking Krishna why he was chosen to kill his own cousins. Krishna says "You see them as kith and kin, I on the other hand am tasked with upholding Dharma and will do whatever it takes to accomplish this." One can argue if Adharma (opposite of Dharma) was committed to uphold Dharma. He was a brilliant manipulator, strategist, enforcer of all that is good in this world, and he died like any mortal would; in insignificance.

BHAGAVAD GITA

The *Bhagavad Gita* is part of the *Mahabharata* epic. This part is a dialogue of about 45 minutes between Krishna and Arjuna that takes place right before the Kurukshetra battle. Just before the battle, Arjuna raised concerns about the morality of imminent violence. Krishna reminded Arjuna of his *Accountability* from the core philosophies of the *Upanishads* and other Hindu texts.

Bhagvad Gita remains moral and spiritual guidance compass for many in India and the world, even today.

YUDHISHTHIRA

The eldest of the Pandavas, who was older than even Duryodhana, as per the custom of the country, was supposed to be the next ruler. However, the king, Dhritarashtra, never wanted that to happen while he could never state that honestly. Therefore, he surreptitiously encouraged Duryodhana to move against Pandavas.

ARJUNA

Arjuna was one of the five Pandava brothers of the Mahabharata epic. Born to Kunthi and and King Pandu had having the energy of Indra, the leader of the Gods. At a very young age he got acclaim for his sincerity and skill in archery. He was known for his steadfastness and single mindedness in pursuing his goals. He was instrumental in winning Draupadi in a contest for himself and his brothers as their joint wife. He also married Subhadra the sister of Krishna and Balarama and kept his friendship with them for ever. Lord Krishna became his mentor and guide for the rest of his life.

DURYODHANA

Duryodhana, the eldest son of Kaurava's, was envious of his cousins the Pandavas from childhood itself. He grew up to be an evil and wicked person. He was always looking for ways to remove the Pandavas owing to their strength, fame and popularity among the people of the kingdom. Pandavas, on the other hand, excelled in almost everything, especially in the use of weapons. Pandavas were always victorious in studies as well as in games. Duryodhana once also tried to kill Bhima, the physically strongest amongst Pandavas, by throwing him into the river, but his plan failed.

SHAKUNI

Shakuni was the prince of Gandhara Kingdom, later to becoming the King after his father's death. He is the main antagonist in the Mahabharata. He was the brother of Gandhari and hence Duryodhana's maternal uncle. He was proficient in the game of dice and instrumental in Duryodhana's personality.

THE MARRIAGE OF DRAUPADI – WIFE OF FIVE HUSBANDS

During the hiding, one of the Pandavas, Arjuna participated in a swaymavaram ceremony (a contest for choosing a husband) that was conducted by King Drupada of Panchala Kingdom, for his daughter Draupadi, also known as "Panchali." Arjuna won the contest and brought Draupadi to the Pandavas' house.

After reaching home, they told their mother, Kunthi "We have brought home something special. Come and see" Like a typical Indian mother, she responded by saying "Share it amongst yourselves," As per tradition, mother's words were like a law to them, so Draupadi was 'shared' amongst all five brothers as their wife.

That incident made Kaurava's and Duryodhana come to know that Pandava's, were alive. While Duryodhana wanted to wipe out Pandavas, the elders advised giving half of the kingdom to the Pandavas as a conciliation.

THE GAME OF CHATHURANGA

To confer the title of emperor to Yudhishthira, the Pandavas conducted a Rajasooyam. This instigated Kauravas further, and they wanted to end the Pandavas. Fully aware that they can't do it openly, as the Pandavas are incomparable in strength and weaponry.

Duryodhana went to his maternal uncle Shakuni to seek advice. Shakuni suggested Duryodhana invite Yudhishtira and other Pandavas for a game of chaturanga. Yudhishtira agreed to participate and miserably failed in the game. He not only lost his kingdom and all valuable possessions; he even lost his brothers and wife Draupadi in it.

After the game was over, as per the game conditions, Pandavas became the slaves of the Kauravas. Dussasana, younger brother of Duryodhana, dragged Draupadi to the court by her hair. While all the elders protested, he did not heed to anyone. Duryodhana also prodded Dussasana to disrobe Draupadi in the court. Draupadi prayed to her lord brother, Krishna, to rescue her from humiliation. Lord Krishna ensured that Draupadi's saree remains endless and Dussasana gets exhausted in pulling it. Draupadi took a vow in the court that she would not tie her hair till she dressed it with Dussasana's blood.

THE PANDAVAS' EXILE

Dhritarashtra finally intervened and advised the Pandavas to go into exile for 12 years. As per the condition, in the 13th year, they could stay in any inhabited place, hidden from Kauravas; if they are found, they will have to go back into the exile for another 12 years.

THE GREAT BATTLE OF KURUKSHETRA

It turned out that the great Kurukshetra war was the only option left. Duryodhana sought Krishna's army, and Pandavas requested for himself to be with them since both of them were his relatives. While the war lasted for eighteen days only, but the myth is that it wiped out 80% of the male population from India.

It killed all the Kauravas. The destruction caused by the war was unthinkable. All the seniors who were left alive after the war, Dhritarashtra, Gandhari, Kunthi and Vidur, took the path of Vanaprastham (living the rest of their life in the forests till death).

Printed in Great Britain
by Amazon